HOW TO BE A PROFESSIONAL GAME MASTER

The Ultimate Guide to Building a Successful Career as a Professional Game Master

GM David C.

ISBN: 9798866441860

Printed in the United States of America

HOW TO BE A PROFESSIONAL GAME MASTER: THE ULTIMATE GUIDE TO BUILDING A SUCCESSFUL CAREER AS A PROFESSIONAL GAME MASTER

AUTHOR'S PREFACE

Welcome, brave souls and imaginative minds, to a volume dedicated solely to pursuing professional excellence in game mastering. While countless resources are available to hone your skills as a dungeon master, game master, or storyteller, this book is specifically tailored for those looking to take their passion to the next level—by making it a profession.

You may have encountered seminal works like "The Monsters Know What They're Doing" or resources like Sly Flourish's "The Lazy DM." If you haven't, I recommend delving into these treasure troves. These works' techniques, strategies, and perspectives will make you a better game master. As professionals, we should be on a continuous quest for excellence, ever seeking to enhance the quality of our sessions.

However, the leap from an excellent game master to a professional one involves more than storytelling skills or rulebook mastery. It's about providing an invaluable service, an unforgettable experience that players are happy to pay for. That's where this volume comes in. The advice, best practices, and professional insights shared in these pages are designed to help you navigate the myriad challenges and opportunities of turning your passion for game mastering into a career.

The most important tenet of professional game mastering is placing the players' needs and desires at the forefront. You are not just crafting an adventure; you are also providing entertainment, friendship, and sometimes even therapy. Each player is entrusting you with something precious: their time and imagination. Remember this as you make decisions, both big and small, about how to run your sessions.

As you read this book, I hope you will find the inspiration, knowledge, and courage needed to step into this fascinating and ever-evolving career. Whether you're considering running your first paid session or you've been at this for years and want to up your game, welcome to the extraordinary journey of being a professional game master.

May your tables be ever full, and your stories never end.

DM David C.

An Old Grognard in a New Age of Gaming

THE GAME MASTER
WHO CHANGED LIVES

FORWARD BY
KURT FRANK

When I first picked up a set of polyhedral dice and skimmed through the rulebook of a popular tabletop role-playing game, I was gripped by a sense of wonder. The possibilities seemed endless like entire universes had suddenly unfurled before me, awaiting exploration. I convinced a group of friends to embark on this journey with me, eagerly taking on the role of the Game Master. We began our campaign with hearts full of excitement, only to realize that our sessions lacked a certain... magic. It was as if we were musicians with all the right instruments but couldn't find the rhythm to create a symphony. Despite our initial enthusiasm, our campaign faltered, and the magic that should have bound us in this new communal experience began to wane.

That's when we discovered David, a professional Game Master who offered to guide us through our adventure. Skeptical but hopeful, we agreed, and that decision changed our lives.

From the moment David unfolded the map and began to narrate our story, it was evident that this was a different league of game mastering. The landscapes were vivid, the challenges were meticulously crafted, and the narrative was so compelling that we found ourselves living the lives of our characters between sessions. David's skill breathed life into a campaign that had been merely limping along. As we battled dragons and navigated political intrigue, we became heroes in a living, breathing world —a world that David orchestrated with the skill of a maestro.

And something remarkable happened. Our campaign didn't just flourish; it transformed into an epic saga that bound us together as lifelong friends. The lines between player and character blurred, and we grew, not just in the game but as individuals. We became more empathetic, more creative, more strategic, and, most of all, more connected. Birthdays, holidays, and significant life events became shared celebrations and milestones in our collective journey. When we faced challenges in our real lives, we tackled them with the same collaborative spirit we employed to defeat formidable in-game foes.

It was no longer just a game; it was a shared odyssey that enriched our lives in immeasurable ways, thanks to a professional Game Master who knew how to turn dice and character sheets into an experience of profound personal and communal growth.

This book aims to equip you with the skills to become a transformative Game Master like David, who doesn't just oversee a game but crafts experiences that leave a lasting impact on people's lives. It's a calling, a vocation that's as demanding as it is rewarding. If you wish to be a professional game master, remember you have the potential to create not just games but memories, not just campaigns but lifelong friendships.

As you delve into the subsequent chapters, may you find the tools, techniques, and inspiration to elevate your passion into a fulfilling and financially rewarding profession. David showed us how a truly great Game Master can change lives; now it's your turn to roll the dice and do the same.

Here's to your journey. May it be epic.

Best Wishes, Kurt

INTRODUCTION: THE JOURNEY TO BECOMING A PROFESSIONAL GAME MASTER

Welcome to a roadmap unlike any other—a guide designed to propel you into a world where storytelling meets business acumen, where imagination pairs with pragmatism, and where your passion for tabletop role-playing games can transform into a flourishing career. Yes, you read that correctly. You can make a career, a good one at that, as a professional Game Master. How good? With dedication and commitment, you can apply the methods and strategies described in the upcoming chapters to potentially earn a weekly income of over $2000 from the comfort of your own home.

Some might scoff at the idea, dismissing tabletop role-playing as mere "play" or trivial escapism. Don't let the skeptics mislead you; being a professional Game Master is a serious business that demands a unique blend of skills. You are not merely an overseer of fantasy realms. You are a storyteller, a community manager, an event planner, a businessperson, and even a pseudo-psychologist who helps players unravel their deepest desires and fears within a fictional setting.

THE TRUTH OF THE PROFESSIONAL GAME MASTER MARKET

It's Real Work

Let's get one thing straight: this is real work. Setting up complex narratives, designing balanced challenges, tailoring experiences to individual players, scheduling sessions, and promoting your services consume time, energy, and creative willpower. Unlike amateur sessions you may run casually, a professional endeavor will continuously push you to upgrade your abilities. Like any other vocation, this one comes with administrative duties, customer relations, and the need for constant upskilling. Yet, if approached with diligence and commitment, it can be as financially and emotionally rewarding as any other career you might contemplate.

Personal and Professional Fulfillment

Imagine waking up each day excited to dive into worlds that exist on the horizon of your creativity. Imagine your players' smiles, gasps, and applause as they traverse through unimaginable challenges, achieve significant milestones, or survive cliffhangers—all guided by your narrative prowess. Your impact on people's lives is not superficial; you offer an escape, a platform for self-discovery, and a social framework that fosters friendships and teamwork.

The emotional rewards are unparalleled, but you should consider the professional benefits. You'll build a portfolio, create a personal brand, and even partner with gaming companies or platforms. You're not just entering a career; you're joining a community that respects artistry, values your skills, and offers endless possibilities for growth.

In my early days as a professional Game Master, I had the remarkable opportunity to bring together a group of strangers from various countries and time zones into a realm of imagination. They came from all walks of life, unified only by their interest in role-playing games. I was initially nervous; this was my first professional campaign, and the pressure to perform well was immense. But the moment we started our session zero, something magical happened.

Every week, like clockwork, they met in our designated online space. Time differences didn't matter; it was as if the real world paused, and we were all transported to a world where halflings, dragons, dwarves, humans, goblins, and orcs roamed. The campaign I designed was an expansive, immersive journey that started with them as fledgling adventurers and saw them growing into figures of epic proportions.

Over nearly three years, their characters evolved from level 1 to the pinnacle of their power at level 20. But it wasn't just about leveling up or acquiring magical items but about the stories we crafted together. They faced moral dilemmas, took down corrupt leaders, saved entire cities, and thwarted apocalyptic scenarios. The culmination was an earth-shattering, realms-shaking finale that had them going toe-to-toe with entities so powerful that even gods would think twice before intervening.

In those two and a half years, something else happened: they became true friends. Outside the game, they started sharing news about their lives, celebrating each other's successes, and offering a shoulder to lean on in difficult times. What began as a client-GM relationship blossomed into a fellowship that will last a lifetime. They came for the game but stayed for the friendships that formed, the shared laughter and tears, the thrill of victory, and the agony of defeat. They now had a catalog of shared experiences, of epic tales that were theirs and theirs alone.

And to think, all of this came to be because they took a chance on hiring a professional Game Master.

In retrospect, the value of what we created goes beyond the game board, the dice rolls, and the character sheets. It's about the power of storytelling to bridge gaps between cultures, transcend time zones, and forge connections that are as real as any you'd find outside the gaming table. And for a Game Master, professional or otherwise, I believe there's no more significant achievement.

The following chapters will explain everything you need to know to turn this vision into reality. From honing your storytelling techniques to managing your financials, from setting up your digital platforms to customer engagement, this book is your comprehensive guide to turning professional in a field that combines the best of imaginative play and business.

So grab your dice, notepads, and most expansive dreams as we embark on this extraordinary journey to transform you from a passionate hobbyist into a consummate professional Game Master. Are you ready to roll?

Let's begin.

CHAPTER 1:
THE POWER OF
PROFESSIONALISM

You Can Be A Professional Game Master.

I can remember exactly where I was when I first read the phrase, "professional game master." It was 2003, and I was at my desk in the office where I wrote programs and managed servers for a manufacturing firm. The "day job." A job that I had been at for years, and frankly I was often bored. So here I was, reading about somebody who was calling themselves a "Professional Game Master," and claiming that this was a full-time job. And my mind exploded!

If you picked up this book, then you are probably just like me, and can recall the moment when the bomb went off in your head. "Professional Game Master." Professional! A dream job, right? But perhaps just for the one in a million person who just happens to live in a huge market such as New York or L.A. where professional dog walkers and other such luxury dream jobs thrived?

And so it was, for most of us, just a pipe dream. But that was before the advent and spread of online tabletop gaming, and the rise of the Live Action Role Play.

The Adventure Zone began in 2006, Acquisitions Inc. In 2008, and Critical Role in 2012, launching just as Twitch and other streaming services were attracting the greatest attention. At the same time virtual tabletop software that could connect players online was emerging in the early aughts, with Fantasy Grounds launching in 2004, Roll20 in 2012, and FoundryVTT and the ever-important Discord both launching in 2015.

Players who could not find a home group to live out their own adventures increasingly turned to the internet to find like-minded folks, and the explosion of these services created a new kind of gamer and a huge market for professional game masters. By the year 2020, these technologies were ripe when the largest challenge to tabletop gaming occurred. Restrictions on gatherings during the COVID pandemic resulted in canceled in-person events worldwide, and the explosion of the demand that was met by an influx of a new class of professional game masters. I was one of those game masters.

I had plans to attend Gary Con XII in Lake Geneva, Wisconsin, on March 26-29th, 2020. This was a long-time dream of mine, to attend the convention honoring the work and life of Gary Gygax, co-creator of Dungeons and Dragons. Not only was I going to Lake Geneva to play great adventures, I had a ticket to play a session of an original Greyhawk dungeon in Gary Gygax's house. The very first game of D&D was played in his dining room, and we would be playing in that room at the same table! This was a dream come true, and I was over the moon for weeks, bragging about my fortune to people who mostly didn't understand or care.

But the news was not looking good in late March of 2020. I heard that SXSW was canceled and that the NCAA basketball games were being canceled, my gut clenched, and I realized my dream was in jeopardy. Then 7 days before the convention, the announcement came. Gary Con XII, 2020 was canceled.

However, this huge demand came with some problems, such as sub-standard GM services offered by groups I like to refer to as "Dungeon Mills." You know the ones that have many, many listings across the online platforms and offer every popular adventure at every possible time period. All are listed under one name, yet you don't always get the same GM because the boss is handling multiple accounts and then feeding the games which are booked to a pool of poorly prepared "professional GMs" who quite often are reading and running that particular adventure for the first time ever, resulting in lackluster delivery, huge amounts of dead air, and a shaky grasp on the basic elements of the game. There have been many miserable posts on Reddit about such shameful, low-quality "Dungeon Mill" outfits.

My goal here is to offer my best advice on delivering top-quality service as a professional game master. By doing your best to provide a smooth, high quality and satisfying experience to your player, you help not only your players, but yourself and all of your cohorts in this nascent field. Because the quality of service that you provide ultimately reflects on all of us who consider ourselves to be professional game masters.

Much of my grounding in professionalism comes from my experience as a technology manager. Still, much of it is simply a matter of acting with integrity in everything I do and say, with a belief that my hard work and integrity are essential for the best results. My integrity requires that I thoroughly study the rules and material that I intend to present, provide a safe, collaborative space for my players, and observe and respond to their needs while safeguarding their agency.

In these chapters, I will delve into many job particulars, such as how to market your game sessions and recruit new players, how to run the games, including an all-important session zero, and how to leverage the best technology has to offer to offer the best game experience and keep it human-based. But this first chapter is the one in which we grapple with the very concept of the professional game master. I am sure you will have heard disparaging remarks about the idea of someone paying to play a game when the long history of tabletop role-playing games revolves around small groups of friends playing as a hobby. I do not deny that I even had such a reaction the first time I heard of the concept of paying to play.

Ain't Nothing In This World For Free

That first article I read in 2003 was titled "Professional Dungeon Master? You're Kidding, Right?" The very idea seemed aberrant to the great ranks of hobby gamers at the time. GMing was often seen as a chore, and players often rotated in that role. Other groups were built by dedicated GMs who performed the work from love of the game. Snacks or Pizza for the GM are often touted as token recompense for the game master's time and expense (as the GM is usually buying the books, terrain, maps, etc.)

First, we will grapple with answering the question, "Why a professional game master?" The simplest answer that I can offer is simple supply side economics: excessive demand. There are far more people who wish to play tabletop role-playing games than there are skilled game masters capable of providing space for them all for free. Free tables are around but are generally insular sects of friends who have more people who want to join than places at their tables. They can pick and choose from a ready pool of players looking to get into a campaign for free.

Game Master As Referee.

In the beginning, every game is a hobby. Eventually, some of these games become sports. Sport moves a game into the realm of entertainment. If people will pay to get into a stadium to watch the local player's pitch baseballs, eventually, it becomes desirable to attract the best players to your ball park, so you pay them. And of course if you are paying the players, you will be paying their coaches, and the people who officiate the games, umpires, or referees. This is well accepted but of course there is a viable business model behind it, the fans who wish to be entertained and will part with their money for the pleasure.

In the sprawling world of tabletop role-playing, sometimes even the most passionate groups find themselves stranded in the desert of creative stagnation. To illustrate the game-changing impact a professional Game Master can make, let's delve into the story of the Sundered Shields, a group of enthusiastic but directionless adventurers.

THE TURNING POINT: FROM FANTASY STRUGGLERS TO ADVENTURERS EXTRAORDINAIRE

The Struggle

The Sundered Shields had been friends since high school. Their sacred gaming nights grew infrequent and lackluster as adulthood unfolded with responsibilities—jobs, families, and other commitments. Each tried to be the Game Master, but their campaigns seemed flat. Their characters often end up in uninspired quests, meandering without a clear objective or emotional weight. The fantasy world they occupied felt more like a haphazard collection of clichés than an immersive experience. Everyone loved the idea of the game but felt the magic wane as the years passed. Was it simply nostalgia, they wondered, that made them remember their early campaigns as epically adventurous and emotionally resonant?

The Turning Point

As a last-ditch effort, they pooled their resources and hired a professional Game Master. After researching various platforms and profiles, they settled on Elena, a seasoned pro with glowing reviews and a portfolio that boasted a mix of traditional high fantasy and complex character-driven narratives.

The Flourishing Campaign

From the very first session, they realized what they'd been missing. Everyone knew they were in for something special from the moment Eleanor began. Her storytelling was rich, her characters vivid, and her world-building astonishingly intricate. Yet, what stood out the most was her ability to create tailored challenges and arcs for each character, making every player feel essential to the story.

Eleanor brought expert storytelling and a deep understanding of pacing, suspense, and emotional stakes. She populated their world with morally complex characters, political intrigue, and realistic economies. The monsters they faced were not just bags of hit points but intricate beings with their agendas. Eleanor incorporated each character's backstory into the central plot, making every party member feel vital to the campaign.

Under Eleanor's guidance, the Sundered Shields navigated treacherous dungeons and brokered political alliances. They faced moral quandaries that left them questioning their characters' most profound beliefs. And each week, as they sat down to play, whether in person or virtually, the group became more invested in the world and each other.

Eleanor introduced them to a higher form of play, transcending mere dice-rolling and rule-quoting. She taught them the true essence of storytelling and its power to foster genuine human connections.

Lifelong Friendships Forged

In a short time, the Sundered Shields went from a group on the verge of disbandment to a dedicated team of heroes immersed in a fantastical universe. Not only did their characters grow stronger, braver, and more nuanced, but so did their real-world friendships. Eleanor's guidance didn't just improve their gaming experience; it enriched their interpersonal dynamics. Arguments turned into constructive debates, and individual disappointments transformed into collective triumphs.

As the campaign flourished, so did their friendships. The group used the game to explore personal challenges and celebrate individual growth. They integrated milestones like birthdays, job promotions, and life events into the narrative as feast days or quests. Eleanor's professionalism made room for something even more valuable: a rekindling of genuine emotional connection between the Sundered Shields.

Today, not only does the group fervently await each session as a highlight of their week, but their strengthened friendships also spill into other aspects of life. They've become each other's confidantes, a tight-knit community bound by the shared adventures in a world rendered vivid by a professional's touch.

Years later, the group still fondly recalls their transformative adventure under Eleanor's stewardship. This experience led to lifelong friendships and an unwavering love for the world of fantasy role-playing. They remained clients of Eleanor for several campaigns, but her impact on them transcended any particular game; she had turned them into a family united by a shared journey through magical lands and moral complexities.

The Takeaway

The transformation of the Sundered Shields from a languishing group into an invigorated team of adventurers speaks volumes about the power of a professional Game Master. By elevating the craft of game mastering into a full-fledged profession, you offer something invaluable: a space for people to connect, imagine, and grow.

In this career, your skills don't just build campaigns; they build communities. The ability to bring about this kind of magic is a testament to the impact that a professional Game Master can have. So, as you venture into this field, remember you're not just rolling dice and reciting lore. As Eleanor did for the Sundered Shields, you're crafting experiences that can change lives.

Eleanor's impact is one example of how becoming a professional can elevate the game and the lives entangled in its intricate narrative webs. It is a testament to the profound potential awaiting those who dare to journey into the professional realm of Game Mastering. This profession doesn't merely entertain but enriches lives in seen and unseen ways.

SETTING EXPECTATIONS :

THE FINANCIAL BREAKDOWN FOR A PRO GM

The Dream Scenario

Imagine a week where you've scheduled a maximum of 40 hours of gaming. You have a stable roster of six players, each willing to pay $10 an hour for your expert game mastering. Here's how the math breaks down:

6 players x $10/hour = $60/hour

$60/hour x 40 hours/week = $2,400/week

$2,400/week x 4 weeks/month = $9,600/month

Wow, $9,600 a month, working from home doing something that you love? Sounds like a dream! But let's bring some reality into the equation.

The Reality Check

Recruitment and Setup: A significant portion of your time will go into recruiting players, planning sessions, and setting up the game. These hours are often unpaid, effectively reducing your hourly rate.

Fluctuating Income: Player turnover, cancellations, and other disruptions mean your income will be inconsistent. It's risky to rely on this as your sole source of income.

Community Norms: Today, professional GMs make around $5 per player per hour, roughly half the dream rate mentioned above. The community needs to work together to uplift the value of professional GMing.

Expenses: Subscriptions to virtual tabletop platforms, premium modules, props, and possibly even self-employment taxes can take a significant bite out of your earnings.

The Collective Uplift

These dream numbers can tempt you to price your services higher, but remember, there's a delicate balance between what you offer and what players are willing to pay. At the same time, I caution professional GMs not to undercut their peers and instead choose a reasonable fee that reflects the value your services provide. As the saying goes, "A rising tide lifts all boats." The professional GM community benefits when everyone is transparent about their fees and values their time appropriately. Over time, this can normalize higher rates across the board.

Similarly, I discourage new GMs from giving away their product for free. In my first several months running weekly campaigns on a popular online platform I offered new players a free first session. Of course, I had a lot of takers, but very few of these players returned as paying members of the group. When trying to build a weekly campaign with a stable party, it was unfair to my other players to keep introducing new players into the campaign for what would almost always prove to be a one-shot for them.

On the other hand, I highly encourage new GMs to practice their craft with free playtest sessions. These are usually run as a free one-shot, as you are tuning up a new adventure or learning on a new VTT. In this case you will want to offer your sessions for free and be transparent about the purpose of the session. This will allow you to gain experience without the total pressure of running a paid session.

Most professional GMs today supplement their income with another job. However, it's possible to make a full-time living from game mastering with hard work, effective self-promotion, and applying best practices like those outlined in this manual. Just remember, like any other profession, it will require dedication, business acumen, and much heart.

In the following chapters, we will dig deeper into the practical aspects of game mastering, offering techniques to make your world as vivid and transformative as the ones we've explored today. But first, we will delve into the importance of Session Zero and the use of safety tools to be an effective game master. Stay tuned because the journey is only just beginning.

CHAPTER 2:
THE CRITICAL IMPORTANCE OF SESSION ZERO — CONSENT, SAFETY TOOLS, AND SETTING EXPECTATIONS

For many, the term "Session Zero" might sound like an unnecessary preamble to the actual game. Actually, it's the foundation upon which successful and inclusive campaigns are built. As a professional Game Master, it's your responsibility not just to entertain but also to create a safe, respectful environment for all players. This chapter will cover how to effectively manage Session Zero, focusing on fostering a cohesive party by making a safe space for all players. This includes consent in RPG gaming, popular safety tools like lines and veils, and the X card.

CONSENT IN
RPG GAMING

The Consent Form

A consent form can serve as a clear, written record of what topics or scenarios are off-limits. This might include graphic violence, sexual content, or specific phobias like spiders or heights. Players can indicate their comfort level with various topics, allowing you to tailor the campaign accordingly. Some professionals even offer this form digitally before the session, allowing players to fill it out privately.

Open Discussion

It's important to discuss the consent form verbally as well. This offers a chance for players to explain their choices and for everyone to understand the boundaries set by their fellow adventurers.

POPULAR RPG SAFETY TOOLS

Lines And Veils

Lines are topics or actions that are entirely off the table and should not appear in the game.

Veils are elements that can exist in the game world but will not be explicitly described or will happen "off-screen."

For example, a player might set a line against sexual assault and a veil against torture. As the GM, you would then know not to introduce any mention of the elements in the first case and only to imply or vaguely reference to the second.

The X Card

A player can activate this physical or digital "card" whenever a game's content becomes uncomfortable for them. It serves as an immediate signal to the Game Master to navigate away from the current scenario or topic, no questions asked. This tool provides a non-verbal way for players to express discomfort without significantly breaking the flow of the game.

Additional Tools And Research

While lines and veils and the X card are popular and effective, they're not the end of our development in safety. Tools like Script

Change, the OK Check-In, and many others offer additional layers of safety and comfort. Because this chapter can't cover all the available tools, it's essential for you, as a professional Game Master, to continue your education. Becoming conversant in a wide array of safety tools equips you to handle diverse and dynamic player groups. It makes you more marketable as a considerate and knowledgeable professional.

See the Appendix for more resources.

Session Zero: Setting Expectations

"Session Zero" is not just a trendy term; it's a foundational element of successful campaigns. This is the time to discuss what everyone wants from the campaign— whether that be a combat-heavy dungeon crawl, a politically charged court drama, or a wilderness exploration adventure.

Player Preferences

It's crucial to understand what each player is looking to experience. Some may thrive in combat scenarios, while others find joy in character-to-character dialogues or world exploration.

Crafting The Blend

Once you understand individual preferences, you can tailor the campaign to feature a balanced mix of combat, social interactions, and exploration.

Open Communication

Encourage players to voice their feelings about the campaign as it progresses. The Session Zero conversation should be ongoing, allowing you to adjust the balance of elements as you go.

Forging A Cohesive Party Through Character Creation

In a professionally run game, character creation isn't just about rolling dice and figuring out your character's statistics—it's also about creating a cohesive party dynamic. While your players' characters might have vastly different backgrounds, classes, or even races, they will be adventuring together and need a reason to do so. As a professional Game Master, you can facilitate a smoother, more engaging campaign by helping players establish pre-existing connections or "bonds" during character creation.

You can begin Session Zero by talking about your desire to work with a group that agrees to the conceit they are an adventuring party. You may even explain that you wish to avoid seeing characters with tropes such as the Edgelord, Lone Wolf or Mary Sue.

Red Flags During Character Creation

As a professional Game Master, you are responsible for creating a harmonious and enjoyable gaming experience for all your players. Character creation is often the first indication of potential issues that could disrupt the balance and enjoyment of your game. Here are some common red flags to look out for:

The Lone Wolf Or Edgelord

You've probably encountered this player before: they want to create a character shrouded in mystery and work alone, often disrupting the party dynamic. These characters often become a storytelling black hole, drawing too much focus and making collaboration difficult.

Characters designed to be aloof, disconnected, or overly dark can be problematic in a collaborative storytelling experience.

These archetypes often eschew teamwork and can create tension within the group. While it's okay to have a mysterious or somewhat brooding character, it's essential that they can function within a team setting. Encourage such a player to choose at least one other player's character to form a bond, even if it is a secret, such that they vow never to let them out of their sight.

The Mary Sue

Suppose a player wants to create a virtually flawless character, incredibly skilled at nearly everything. In that case, you might have a Mary Sue on your hands. This archetype is a well-rounded character that is excessively perfect, lacking in flaws, and built to be exceptional in nearly every way; enabling a "Main Character Syndrome" can disrupt the game's balance, overshadow other characters, and take away from the collaborative nature of the game.

A great way to deal with a player building a Mary Sue is to say, "I know that you are a great role player, so I'd like to challenge you to build some flaws into Mary Sue."

The Overpowered (Op) Or Exploit Character

Watch out for players who seem more interested in exploiting rules than in crafting a compelling story or character. This player has spent hours combing through rulebooks and online forums to find the perfect combination of race, class, and feats to make an overpowered character. They often push the boundaries of rules to the limit, disrupting the game's balance.

Whether multi-classing to an extreme or utilizing questionable "rule hacks," these players can unbalance the game and make it less fun for others. And often you as the GM may not see the exploit in the build until they unleash it in game with great glee. Here, it takes the grace of the good Game Master to manage the player's expectations. Rules debates are not fun. Suggesting that "We'll play it your way and see how it goes today, and delve into the rules later," is an excellent way to keep the flow of the game going and yet assert a right to over-rule the next game, with full examination of the rules. Also, there is nothing wrong with making a GM ruling based on your gut. I have said "I just don't feel that was the way the rules intended this to work, and so we are going to have to agree to disagree on this one in my game world."

Mitigating Power Gaming

Use standardized character creation rules, like the Standard Array or Point Buy systems in D&D 5E, to ensure a balanced and fair game and no one is overpowered.

Unintended Rule Interpretations

Be cautious of players who seem to have "found" rules online that stretch or expand abilities in ways that the game designers did not intend. Always refer back to the source material. Be cautious of players who cite obscure online sources or who interpret rules in a way that significantly boosts their character's abilities. Always cross-reference with official materials and clarify any misinterpretations. Trust your judgment as the GM.

Introduce Flaws

Encourage your players to design characters with flaws. Not only does this provide a more balanced experience, but it also allows for richer character development and storytelling opportunities. One way to humanize a character and integrate them into the narrative is to encourage the incorporation of character flaws. These flaws can serve as great role-playing hooks and provide opportunities for character growth.

Being proactive at the character creation stage can save you many headaches down the road. You can preemptively address many issues that could become problems later on. By establishing a few ground rules and keeping an eye out for these red flags, you can help ensure a balanced and enjoyable experience for everyone involved. Your goal is to facilitate an enjoyable, fair game for everyone involved, and that starts with balanced and well-thought-out characters.

Why Bonds Matter

Bonds serve as a narrative glue that holds the party together. They offer in-game reasons for characters to interact, make decisions, and collaborate. In the heat of battle or during crucial decision-making moments, these bonds can tip the balance and add depth and realism to the role-playing experience.

Facilitating Bonds

During Session Zero, encourage your players to think about their characters' relationships to each other, the world, and important NPCs. This can be done through open discussion or by asking specific questions aimed at discovering these connections.

Examples Of Potential Bonds

Here are some sample bonds that can tie characters together:

Sibling Rivalry: Two characters are siblings, always trying to one-up each other but ultimately having each other's backs.

Mentor and Protégé: One older character has taken a younger

character under their wing.

Battle Buddies: Two characters served in the same military unit and trust each other implicitly.

Old Friends: Two or more characters grew up in the same village and have been friends since childhood.

Debt of Honor: One character saved another's life, and that character feels a life debt.

Secret Knowledge: Two characters share information about a mysterious artifact or hidden enemy that others do not know about.

Romantic Interest: Two characters have a budding romance or unspoken feelings for each other.

Business Partners: Characters are in a mutually beneficial, albeit primarily financial, relationship.

Bound by Quest: All characters have sworn to fulfill the same quest or prophecy.

Reformed Enemies: Two characters were once enemies but now fight for a common cause.

Encouraging your players to create bonds between their characters sets the stage for a rich and engaging campaign where interpersonal dynamics add as much to the story as any dungeon crawl or epic battle.

Concluding Thoughts

Remember, your primary goal is to create a fun, engaging experience that is also respectful and safe for all participants. Bonds, consent and safety tools are not about limiting your storytelling potential; they're about ensuring that your stories are inclusive and enjoyable for everyone at the table.

In the following chapters, we will explore further nuances

of professional game mastering, including advanced narrative techniques and business considerations. But at the heart of your professional endeavor should always be a commitment to player safety and enjoyment. Session Zero is where that commitment begins.

SAFETY TOOLS AT WORK: THE NIGHT SAFETY TOOLS SAVED THE CAMPAIGN

Jamie had been a professional Game Master for years, and she knew that a big part of her job was understanding her players. She was excited to kick off a new dark fantasy campaign but mindful that the tone could venture into sensitive territory. During Session Zero, she introduced the concept of lines and veils. Her players were a mix of seasoned and new, but all were eager for the campaign to succeed.

Ryan, one of her players, set a hard line against depictions of child harm, while Sarah set a veil on graphic descriptions of gore and violence. Other players had their own lines and veils, and Jamie took careful notes.

Weeks into the campaign, the party found themselves in a haunted, crumbling mansion where they had to rescue an important NPC from a cult performing dark rituals. Jamie had initially planned for them to discover a disturbing scene that, unbeknownst to her during the planning stage, would have crossed Ryan's line.

However, thanks to the lines and veils discussion, she altered the narrative. Instead of a horrifying scene involving child harm, the party uncovered a room filled with unsettling, arcane symbols and evidence of rituals—eerie but not crossing any boundaries. The tension was palpable, but everyone was comfortable enough to continue engaging with the story.

Later in the same session, a combat encounter with the cultists unfolded. Typically, Jamie reveled in detailed, vivid descriptions of the party's battles. But remembering Sarah's veil, she toned down the explicitness of her combat narration. Instead of describing the gore in graphic detail, she used phrases like "Your blade finds its mark" or "The cultist falls, overcome by your attack."

After the session, Sarah and Ryan both expressed how much they enjoyed the adventure. They felt immersed but never uncomfortable, invested but never distressed. It was a moment of professional pride for Jamie, who saw firsthand how the lines and veils safety tools could enhance rather than detract from the storytelling experience. Most importantly, she knew she had succeeded in creating a safe and respectful environment, allowing her players to explore the dark fantasy world she had crafted without fear.

It was a campaign that would go down as one of Jamie's best, not just for its compelling story but also for the sense of trust and mutual respect that allowed her players to fully invest in the narrative. And it all began with a successful Session Zero and the proper application of safety tools.

SAFETY TOOLS AT WORK: THE POWER OF THE X CARD IN ACTION

Michael had been a professional Game Master for several years, always striving to create an inclusive and welcoming table for his players. During Session Zero for his new high-stakes spy thriller campaign, he introduced the concept of the X Card. He explained that if any content made anyone uncomfortable, they could simply display the X Card—either a physical card on the table or a virtual signal in their online interface.

Several sessions into the campaign, the party was deep undercover, infiltrating a high-society gala to gather intelligence. The tension was thick as they navigated through conversations with potentially hostile agents. Michael felt the energy at the table was great—players were engaged, and the story was unfolding dramatically.

However, as he began to introduce a subplot involving an NPC exhibiting predatory behavior towards another character at the gala, Emily, one of his players, activated the X Card. Michael immediately recognized the signal and swiftly transitioned the scene, steering the focus toward another subplot involving a mysterious encrypted message that needed decoding. He moved the narrative along without missing a beat, ensuring the flow of the game remained uninterrupted.

At the end of the session, Michael checked in privately with Emily to make sure she was all right and to inquire about any specific topics he should be aware of for future sessions. Emily thanked him for the swift handling of the situation and explained that the subplot had touched on personal trauma. She was grateful for the X Card, saying that its use helped her continue to enjoy the game without anxiety.

For Michael, the moment reaffirmed why safety tools like the X Card are indispensable, especially for a professional GM. It wasn't just about avoiding discomfort but respecting boundaries and ensuring that the adventures remained enjoyable for everyone involved. The trust between Michael and his players was strengthened that day, all thanks to a simple yet powerful tool and a GM who knew how to use it effectively.

The campaign continued to be a success, with players fully immersed in the world and eagerly looking forward to each session. For Michael, it served as a lesson in the power of empathy and attentiveness, qualities that made him not just a skilled Game Master but a respected professional in his field.

In the next chapter, we'll delve into the logistics of running a campaign, focusing on preparation, time management, and player engagement to ensure your storytelling skills can shine in the best light possible.

CHAPTER 3: RUNNING A PROFESSIONAL SESSION

Managing Time And Progression

As a professional GM, you're not just a storyteller but also a timekeeper. You have a responsibility to ensure that both the action and the story progress at a pace that feels rewarding to your players. Keep an eye on the clock. Suppose you realize that a particular encounter or discussion is taking longer than expected. In that case, you should accelerate events to maintain momentum. Conversely, if things are progressing too quickly, a well-placed obstacle or subplot can slow the pace and allow for more character development.

Bio Breaks

Always pay attention to the importance of breaks. No matter how engrossing the game is, players will appreciate the opportunity to stretch, grab a snack, or use the bathroom. For a 2-hour session, aim for at least one 5-minute break. For a more extended 3-4 hour session, a 10-minute break around the halfway mark is advisable. Announce these breaks in advance so players can anticipate them, enabling them to manage their time and comfort better.

Taking Good Notes

Your notes are your best friend. They help you track important events, decisions made by players, NPC interactions, and clues given. After each session, take a few minutes to jot down key developments and any surprising actions the players took. They will not only help you plan future sessions but also allow you to weave a more intricate and reactive story. Many professional GMs use software to manage their campaign notes. Still, the old pen-and-paper method works just as well, as long as you keep them organized and easily accessible.

By successfully juggling these various elements—time management, player comfort, and note-taking—you'll deliver a seamless and enjoyable experience to your players, increasing their satisfaction and your likelihood of retaining them for future sessions.

Mastering the Art of Combat – Thrills, Strategy, and Efficiency

Introduction

Combat is often the heart-pounding climax of a session, a test of skill and strategy that can mean the difference between glory and ruin for your players. However, keeping these encounters exciting yet smooth-flowing is an art many game masters find challenging. This chapter aims to equip you with the tools and insights needed to run compelling, thrilling combat scenes that will leave your players on the edge of their seats.

Keeping The Action Moving

The first rule of running professional-grade combat is to keep things moving. Nothing kills the tension faster than long pauses and indecisive actions.

Time Limit: Employ a soft timer, 1-2 minutes, for each player to declare their action. A time limit adds a layer of urgency and simulates the split-second decisions made in actual combat scenarios.

Role-play Limit: Limit role-playing during combat rounds to just six words. This limit ensures that the action keeps flowing while allowing for those one-liners and commands that make combat flavorful.

The Battlefield: More Than Just A Grid

An interesting battlefield can make a routine skirmish into a memorable fight. Always consider the following:

Environmental Conditions: Weather, like rain or wind, can affect visibility and movement. Use these conditions to introduce new tactical considerations.

Physical Obstacles: Rocks, trees, or even fallen enemies can serve as cover or hindrance, altering the dynamics of the fight.

Lighting: Shadows and darkness can be manipulated for stealth or to set ambushes, offering creative opportunities for both players and enemies.

Enemy Composition: Variety Is The Spice Of Combat

Your choice of enemies can significantly impact how engaging a combat scenario is.

Mixed Abilities: A mix of spellcasters, tanks, and ranged attackers will force the party to think tactically.

Synergies: Use enemies that can work together in interesting ways, like a necromancer who raises fallen allies or a warrior who gains bonuses when near its commander.

Challenging but Fair: While variety makes combat interesting, it should never feel like a "gotcha!" moment for the players. The enemy's abilities should make thematic and logical sense within the world you've built.

When Retreat Is An Option

Enemies don't always have to fight to the death; intelligent foes might retreat, regroup, or even parley.

Signaling Retreat: Make it clear through description and action when an enemy starts to withdraw. This adds depth and realism.

Tactical Withdrawal: Use retreating enemies to set up future encounters or plot points, turning what could be a simple combat resolution into a continuing narrative.

Non-lethal Outcomes: Sometimes combat can end in capture, negotiations, or a temporary truce. This offers a good change of pace and additional role-playing opportunities down the line.

Conclusion

Running an exciting, streamlined combat session requires preparation, awareness, and a keen understanding of pacing. Implementing the techniques mentioned above can not only make your encounters more enjoyable but also more immersive and memorable. Remember, in the realm of professional game mastering, nothing is more rewarding than hearing your players recount that epic battle weeks or months later as one of their most cherished gaming memories.

Handling Character Death: The Final Chapter in a Hero's Journey

Setting Expectations in Session Zero

During session zero, make sure to discuss the topic of character death openly and transparently with your players. Some players relish the high-stakes nature of a deadly campaign. In contrast, others prefer a more narrative-driven experience with less lethal risks. Establish upfront what happens when a character dies, whether they have options for resurrection or if they'll need to create a new character. This sets the tone for the campaign and avoids future misunderstandings.

The Reality Of Risk And Consequences

In any adventure, risk is an integral part of the experience. It's the balancing force that makes rewards meaningful. Discuss with your players the level of risk they're comfortable with; some may want a gritty, unforgiving world, while others may prefer a more forgiving setting where death is rare but still possible. Make sure this risk level aligns with the expectations set during session zero.

The Moment Of Loss

When a character does meet their end, pause the action. Whether it's a noble sacrifice or an unfortunate roll of the dice, give the character a moment that acknowledges their contributions to the story. This could be a full role-played funeral with eulogies from fellow adventurers, a somber recounting of their greatest feats, or even a heroic epilogue you narrate. This moment not only pays respect to the character but also adds weight to the reality of your game world.

Checking In With The Player

The loss of a character can be emotionally taxing. Always take a moment to privately check in with the player who has lost their character. Acknowledge their feelings and let them know that it's completely normal to feel attached to their character. Offer them options for how they'd like to proceed, whether it's diving back in with a new character immediately or taking a session to be a spectator.

Encouraging A New Beginning

Once the player is ready, encourage them to roll a new character. Sometimes, the end of one story can be the catalyst for an even greater adventure. Offer to spend time outside the regular session to help them integrate their new character into the story, ensuring a smooth transition.

Conclusion

Character death is a significant event that can shape the emotional landscape of your campaign. Handled correctly, it can offer a moment of drama, a chance for reflection, and an opportunity for new beginnings. Always remember, the goal is not to defeat your players but to create a compelling, emotionally rich narrative that everyone will remember for years.

CHAPTER 4: THE LOGISTICS OF BEING A PROFESSIONAL GAME MASTER

So, you've honed your storytelling skills, mastered safety tools, and are now well-versed in the nuances of various gaming systems. But how do you translate these skills into a viable profession? In this chapter, we delve into the logistical aspects of being a professional Game Master, including recruiting players, the differences between in-person and online games, and the ever-tricky topic of scheduling.

The first logistic choice to be made these days is whether your game will be online, or in-person. Each is a great way to share a role playing adventure with a group, but of course they are executed in very different ways, using different tools.

In-Person vs. Online Gaming

In-Person

The tactile experience of rolling physical dice, the direct engagement with players, and the ability to use physical props make in-person games a unique experience. However, these games are geographically limited and may require a dedicated physical space.

Online

Virtual tabletop software like Roll20, Fantasy Grounds, and D&D Beyond have revolutionized the RPG landscape. These platforms offer tools that automate many game mechanics, freeing you to focus on storytelling. Most importantly, you can connect with players worldwide, removing geographical constraints. The downside might be less direct personal engagement and the occasional technical glitch.

I urge the new GM who is learning a new VTT to practice, practice, practice! Please do not subject your paid players to your fits and stumbles with new technology. GMs who cannot operate the technology make a bad name for our profession. Run playtests for free as you figure out the system, and thank your players for helping you become a better GM.

Keep it simple.

As you start out on a new VTT with many features, remember that there is beauty in simplicity. Keep your maps simple at first. Do not feel that you must provide every bell and whistle that technology is capable of at once. Just because you can does not mean you must. Dynamic lighting is great for a dungeon crawl but is not always needed on every map, and in fact is sometimes boring for players who must look at a mostly black screen.

Multitasking Is A Lie!

You might think that running a game on a VTT requires terrific "multitasking" skills. However, when it comes to the term multitasking, I prefer to recognize that it is actually impossible to do two or more things at the same time very well. Instead, I juggle! Right now, I am working on a book I started a little over a month ago. I spent 12 hours on it yesterday and worked until my eyes were too dried out to stare at my screen any longer. My point here is, I cannot write this book and run a game session, any more than I can keep up with the players' ongoing conversation while changing the audio backing track.

I experience multitasking failure all the time when I am running a game on a VTT, and I must do something "in the background." As in, I stop talking or listening to the group as I try to twiddle a checkbox or fill in a name or something, and I leave my players with "the long silence," and at worst they have to ask, "Are you still there?" It is very awkward, and I must apologize and explain that I was off doing something else and get the game back on track. So, I have learned to recognize that multitasking while running a game is nearly impossible for me.

I find it is better to simply ask the players for a moment to take care of something. This signals to the players that they can still converse freely while the GM handles something in the background. Once I am done with the task, I quickly announce when I am back, and the players have my full attention again so we can smoothly slip back into our narrative rhythm.

VIRTUAL TABLETOP SOFTWARE: COMPARISONS AND CHOICES

System , Price , Pros , Cons

Roll20 , Free, Plus $4.17/month or Pro for 8.33/moth

Easy to use, large community, many features and customization options. It can be slow and clunky. GM can host players for free.

Foundry VTT , $50 one-time purchase

Very customizable, great for automation, self-hosted. It can be complex to set up and not have as many features as Roll20 . GM can host players for free.

Fantasy Grounds , $14.99/month

It is very powerful and supports many different RPG systems. It can be expensive and not as user-friendly as Roll20. GMs can host players for free.

Owlbear Rodeo, Free, Fledgling $3.33/month, Bestling $6.66/month

Very lightweight and easy to use, great for beginners, Limited features, not as customizable as other systems. GMs can host players for free.

Tabletop Simulator , $19.99 per user

It is very versatile and can be used for any game. It can be complex to use, not as focused on RPG gaming as other systems. Players must own a copy to use.

Here is a more detailed comparison of each system:

Roll20 is the most popular virtual tabletop system. It is easy to use and has a large community of users. However, it can be slow and clunky and has limited customization options.

Foundry VTT is a newer virtual tabletop system that is gaining popularity. It is very customizable and great for automation. However, it can be complex to set up and has fewer features than Roll20.

Fantasy Grounds is a powerful virtual tabletop system that supports many different RPG systems. However, it can be expensive and less user-friendly than Roll20.

Owlbear Rodeo is a lightweight, easy-to-use virtual tabletop system that is great for beginners. However, it has limited features and is less customizable than other systems.

Tabletop Simulator is a versatile virtual tabletop system that can be used for any game. However, it can be complex to use and is less focused on RPG gaming than other systems.

The best virtual tabletop system for you will depend on your needs and preferences. If you are looking for a simple and easy-to-use system, Roll20 is a good option. If you are looking for a powerful and customizable system, Foundry VTT is a good choice. If you are on a budget, Owlbear Rodeo is a great option. And if you want a versatile system that can be used for any game, Tabletop Simulator is a good choice.

Ultimately, the best way to decide which virtual tabletop system is right for you is to try a few different ones and see which one you like the best.

RECRUITING PLAYERS

In-Person Games

I have used many traditional methods of recruiting players for in-person games, including listings at local game shops, university bulletin boards, and word-of-mouth through social networks. These can be good ways to build up an at-home group, but as a professional, your reach should extend beyond casual meet-ups. I have found great success offering 'teaser' sessions at public events, which can help attract a more dedicated clientele.

Online Games

The digital realm has democratized access to RPGs like never before. Websites, forums, and social media platforms are excellent places to market yourself and your campaigns. A well-curated online presence, complete with samples of your storytelling or glimpses into your game worlds, can attract players from all corners of the globe.

The Scheduling Conundrum

The most daunting logistical challenge for any Game Master, professional or otherwise, is scheduling. As a professional, your income relies on regular, well-attended sessions. Here are some tools to simplify this complex task:

Online Scheduling Tools

Platforms like "When2meet" and "Doodle" can help you and your players find common time slots. These tools allow participants to mark their availability on a shared calendar, making finding a time that works for everyone easier.

Player And Gm Matchmaking Services

Websites like "start playing.games" act as a marketplace for Game Masters and players, offering options to filter by game type, play style, and availability. In addition, platforms like Roll20 and D&D Beyond offer game listings where GMs can advertise their campaigns and recruit players.

Conclusion

Being a professional Game Master is about more than just your skills at the table; it's about leveraging a range of tools and platforms to create a seamless and enjoyable experience for your players—and for you. From recruiting the right players to scheduling sessions, mastering the logistical aspects is crucial for anyone considering game mastering as a profession. With the resources available today, even the most daunting logistical challenges can be managed, letting you focus on what you do best: crafting unforgettable adventures.

CHAPTER 5: THE ART OF SELF-PROMOTION —CRAFTING YOUR PROFESSIONAL BIOGRAPHY AND BEYOND

Start With The Professional Biography

In a crowded marketplace, the first thing that sets you apart is your story, experience, and specific skills. Crafting a compelling professional biography is an essential first step in self-promotion. This isn't just a rundown of your experience; it's your first impression, a gateway to attracting the players you want to engage with. Your bio should succinctly express who you are as a Game Master. Start by detailing your experience in the role-playing world. Mention how long you've been a GM, the types of campaigns you've run, and the game systems you've worked with. Highlight any specialties—such as world-building, storytelling, or character development—that you excel in. Consider sharing numbers like how many campaigns you've completed or how many players you've guided, as these stats lend credibility to your expertise.

Your Experience

How many years have you been gaming? What was your first TTRPG? Have you run long-term campaigns? Here, you'll include any milestones you think would interest potential players or clients, such as completing high-level campaigns, organizing significant gaming events, or even awards you've won in the field.

Specialties

What are the genres or settings you excel at? High fantasy? Cyberpunk? Horror? A well-rounded Game Master is good, but one specializing in particular niches can command higher rates for their expertise.

Systems Supported

Clearly state what gaming systems you are comfortable running. Is it just D&D 5E, or do you also offer Pathfinder, Call of Cthulhu, or Star Wars: Edge of the Empire? Additionally, clarify whether you focus on classic pen-and-paper role-playing or if you also utilize virtual tabletops like Roll20. Describing the gaming environment will help prospective players align their expectations and preferences with your offerings.

Your Style

Describe your game mastering style in a few sentences. Are you more focused on storytelling, or do you prefer mechanics-heavy gameplay? Do you tend to run combat-heavy sessions or lean more towards role-play and puzzles?

What You Bring To The Table

One of the most significant selling points of a professional Game Master is the physical and digital resources and the depth of experience you provide. Players expect a more polished, seamless experience when they're paying for it, and you need to deliver on that front. For example, a premium subscription to Roll20 or DnDBeyond, high-quality microphones, or specialized terrain and miniatures can all be unique selling points. Let's break down some of the essentials you might consider:

Describe any specialized equipment you use to enhance the gaming experience. This could range from custom gaming tables and miniatures to state-of-the-art digital tablets for real-time map editing.

If you use virtual tabletop software like Roll20 or Fantasy Grounds, mention it. Talk about your proficiency with these platforms and how you employ their various features to bring the campaign to life.

If you hold subscriptions to platforms like D&D Beyond, Roll20, or any other resource that allows you to share benefits with your players, highlight this. For example, access to a shared rulebook compendium can be an attractive feature for many players.

If you're subscribed to or support content creators on Patreon or other platforms who produce modules, maps, or other materials you incorporate into your sessions, that's also worth mentioning. It shows your dedication to providing high-quality content for your players.

BEYOND THE BIO: SELF-PROMOTION STRATEGIES

Social Media

Get active on platforms where TTRPG communities thrive. Twitter, Reddit, and specialized forums are excellent places to engage with potential players, answer questions, and show off your expertise. Don't just advertise—contribute meaningfully to discussions.

Networking

Attending local or online events, conventions, or forums can introduce you to potential clients and other game masters. The power of a good recommendation cannot be overstated.

Content Creation

Consider starting a blog, podcast, or YouTube channel where you share tips, stories, or reviews. Not only will this position you as an authority in the field, but it also improves your visibility online.

Testimonials

Nothing sells your services like the words of satisfied players. Collect testimonials after successful campaigns or one-shots and display these prominently on your website or social media.

Packages & Special Offers

Creating different packages can make your services more appealing to a broader audience. Perhaps a discounted rate for a longer commitment or a "newbie" package that includes a short tutorial before the campaign starts.

Setting Your Rates

Look online to gauge the going price for game mastering services. Fees have been on a slow rise, and it's crucial to position yourself competitively. Resist the urge to discount your rates heavily. While it may be tempting to undercut the competition to get your first few clients, doing so only contributes to a race to the bottom in pricing.

By presenting yourself professionally and stating what you offer that others don't, you can command rates that reflect your expertise and the unique flavor you bring to each campaign. Remember, self-promotion is not about bragging; it's about clearly communicating what you can offer to a gaming experience. When done right, it can be the gateway to a fulfilling and profitable career in game mastering.

Conclusion

Self-promotion is an ongoing endeavor. Aside from the above essentials, maintain an active online presence, regularly update your community through social media or newsletters, and always be open to networking opportunities. The role-playing world thrives on community and word-of-mouth, so don't underestimate the power of a satisfied player singing your praises.

CHAPTER 6: THE ART OF RECRUITMENT

Individuals vs. Groups

One of the foundational steps to running a successful campaign as a professional Game Master is the recruitment process. While sometimes you might have the good fortune of being hired by a pre-existing group, you'll often find yourself bringing together individuals who have never met. Both scenarios come with their unique sets of challenges and advantages. This chapter will explore how to navigate these differing landscapes.

THE PRE-EXISTING GROUP

Advantages:

Shared History: A group that already knows each other will have a built-in rapport, shorthand for communication, and likely a common goal in gaming.

Easier to Manage: Planning a campaign that will satisfy everyone might be more manageable because they already know each other's likes and dislikes.

Challenges:

Pre-existing Dynamics: While familiarity is a bonus, this group may also have internal politics or conflicts that you'll have to navigate.

Set Expectations: They may have ingrained expectations from previous experiences and might resist new approaches or styles.

Best Practices:

Initial Meeting: Have a Session Zero to gauge their expectations, styles of play, and any group dynamics you should be aware of.

Regular Check-ins: Even with an established group, it's essential to have regular conversations to ensure everyone remains on the same page.

DAVID CUSACK

INDIVIDUAL PLAYERS MEETING AS STRANGERS

Advantages:

Fresh Start: Since there's no pre-existing group dynamic, you have an opportunity to set the tone and foster a particular kind of group interaction.

Diverse Interests: Individuals might bring a wide range of interests and experiences to the table, offering a rich tapestry for storytelling.

Challenges:

Group Cohesion: Initially, these players may not mesh well, resulting in awkward social interactions or conflicting game objectives.

Time-Consuming: It requires extra time and effort on your part to help them coalesce into a unified team.

Best Practices:

Strong Session Zero: Spend significant time during this session to allow the players to get to know one another. Consider team-building exercises or shared backstory elements to help bond the group.

Ongoing Facilitation: Particularly in the early sessions, you might have to serve as a mediator and facilitator, actively encouraging interaction and guiding the group toward common goals.

Regular Individual Check-ins: Given that this group didn't choose to play with each other initially, regular one-on-ones can be valuable to ensure each player feels heard and included.

Tips for Both Scenarios:

Transparency: Always be clear about your expectations, the campaign's direction, and the type of game you're running.

Openness: Maintain an open channel for feedback, whether with a group or individuals.

Flexibility: Be prepared to adapt. Groups evolve, and individuals find their comfort zones. Your ability to adapt will be crucial in both scenarios.

In Summary

Recruitment can often set the tone for the rest of the campaign. Whether you're dealing with a pre-existing group or assembling a team of individual players, your skill in managing these different scenarios will significantly impact the campaign's success and the satisfaction of your players. Always remember, an excellent Game Master isn't just a storyteller but also a skilled facilitator who can bring people together to create something truly memorable.

CHAPTER 7: TIME, TIME, TIME! HOW TO SCHEDULE EFFECTIVELY

Crafting An Effective Game Listing

Creating an online listing for your game can be both exciting and intimidating. It's your first impression, a pitch that needs to convey not just the basics but also the atmosphere and style of your campaign. Here's a guide to crafting an effective listing for platforms like Roll20:

Title

The title should be catchy but also informative. It's the first thing potential players will see, so make it inviting and indicative of the game's theme or setting.

Good Example: "Mysteries of the Forgotten Kingdom: A High Fantasy Adventure"

Bad Example: "Looking for Players"

Game System And Edition

Clearly state the game system and edition you'll be using. This saves time for players who are looking for something specific.

Example: "Dungeons & Dragons 5th Edition"

Short Description

Write an elevator pitch for your campaign. Aim to encapsulate the essence of the adventure in two or three sentences.

Example: "Journey into the Forgotten Kingdom, a land of ancient mysteries and untold riches. Will you emerge as heroes or become another forgotten tale in the annals of history?"

Long Description

Here, you can expand on the details. Include the type of story, the themes involved, and what players can expect regarding gameplay (combat vs. role-playing, dungeon crawl vs. political intrigue, etc.).

Example: "This campaign will involve heavy exploration and social interaction elements, with combat sprinkled throughout. Expect morally grey choices, complex characters, and intricate world-building."

Session Details

Be very specific about session frequency, expected duration, and time zone. A clearly defined schedule will help players immediately identify if they can commit to the game.

Example: "Weekly sessions on Saturdays, 4-7 PM EST."

Player Experience

Mention what level of experience with tabletop RPGs or the specific system is expected, if any.

Example: "Players of all experience levels are welcome, but a basic understanding of the rules is encouraged."

Safety Tools

Briefly outline any safety tools you'll use, like lines and veils or the X Card. This reassures prospective players that you take their comfort seriously.

Example: "We use the X Card and have a lines and veils discussion during Session Zero."

Application Instructions

Specify how you'd like interested players to apply. Do you want them to message you directly, complete a questionnaire, or join a Discord server for an interview?

Example: "Please send me a private message with your RPG experience and what you hope to get from this campaign."

Taking time to create a thoughtful, comprehensive listing not only helps attract players who are a good fit for your campaign but also sets a professional tone that can help set you apart as a top-tier Game Master.

THE CHALLENGE OF SCHEDULING AND RESCHEDULING IN RPG CAMPAIGNS

Scheduling is often jokingly called the hardest boss in any RPG campaign, and for good reason. Finding a regular slot that works for everyone is no small feat in a world where everyone has their own commitments. As a professional Game Master, you are not just an entertainer but also a scheduler and communicator.

Best Practices For Cancelling Or Rescheduling

Give Advance Notice: The sooner you alert your players to a change, the better. Aim for at least 48 hours' notice when possible.

Be Transparent: Communicate the reason for the change, whether it's a personal emergency, work commitment, or some other issue.

Propose Alternatives: If you need to reschedule, propose multiple new dates and times to accommodate everyone's schedule better.

Confirm Changes: Once a new time has been agreed upon, confirm it with all players and update any shared calendars or scheduling tools you use.

Apologize for the Inconvenience: A simple apology goes a long way. Players set aside time in their busy lives to participate in your game; acknowledging the inconvenience shows you respect their time.

Communication And Commitment

Open lines of communication are crucial. Players should feel comfortable notifying you if they can't make a session. Likewise, you should be proactive in communicating any changes on your end. Consistency is key to a successful long-term campaign, so make sure everyone is committed to the agreed-upon schedule.

Dealing With No-Shows

Immediate Response: If a player fails to show up without prior notice, try to contact them to ensure their safety and to see if they are simply running late.

Proceed with Caution: Depending on the session's structure, you might proceed without the player, giving their character a background role for that session. Never make significant decisions for a missing player's character without their consent.

Post-Session Follow-Up: After the session, follow up with the missing player to discuss their absence. Reiterate the importance of communication for the campaign's success.

Three-Strikes Rule: As a professional, you may opt for a "three-strikes" rule for no-shows. After three unexplained absences, a discussion about continued participation in the campaign becomes necessary.

Remember, as a professional Game Master, your campaign isn't just a casual get-together; it's a commitment that people are investing time and money into. Respecting that commitment, especially when changes are needed, is crucial for maintaining a professional reputation.

CHAPTER 8: VIRTUAL GAMING PLATFORMS AND THE ROLE OF TECHNOLOGY

The internet has revolutionized role-playing games, allowing players and Game Masters to connect from all corners of the world. With many virtual tabletop software at your disposal, it's easier than ever to bring your story to life digitally. However, a cautionary note: technology, if not wielded correctly, can become a hindrance rather than a help.

We touched on these virtual tabletop wares in an earlier chapter, but for review, these are the most common digital tools that professional game masters are using today:

Popular Virtual Tabletop Software

Roll20

A browser-based platform that requires no downloads, Roll20 offers a lot of free assets and functionalities. It's system-agnostic, meaning you can adapt it to various RPG systems.

Fantasy Grounds

This more specialized platform provides specific rule sets and mechanics tailored to a wide array of games. It does require a one-time purchase or a subscription, but the level of customization and automation available can save much time in-game.

Tabletop Simulator

This is a fully 3D environment that simulates a physical tabletop. The learning curve is steeper, but it offers the most tactile experience of all the virtual options.

Other Online Tools

Besided the Virtual Tabletop, tools for managing character sheets and matchmaking tools are very important for a professional game master. Here are the most common tools used for these purposes:

D&D Beyond

Primarily geared toward Dungeons & Dragons 5th Edition, this platform provides various digital tools that help you manage campaigns, including character sheets and rule books. However, it's not a virtual tabletop in the traditional sense.

Start Playing Games

StartPlaying.Games is a great platform for professional GMs to connect with players, manage their bookings, and get paid.

It has an easy to use interface and large community of players. StartPlaying.Games is well-designed and easy-to-use, and most importantly addresses a real need in the TTRPG community. It provides a convenient way for players to find and join games, and handles the financial transactions for you.

StartPlaying.Games is the perfect platform for professional GMs, providing a ready stream of clientele and handling some of the more onerous chores of the professional with a terrific interface.

POTENTIAL PITFALLS OF TECHNOLOGY

Technical Glitches

Nothing ruins immersion faster than a technical glitch at a climactic moment. Unexpected crashes, lags, or software errors can significantly disrupt gameplay.

Complexity Over Narrative

With a range of features and tools, there's a temptation to get carried away, adding flashy effects or complicated mechanics that can detract from the story and characters.

Limited Attention

Screens come with distractions. Browser tabs, notifications, and other applications can lure attention away from the game, affecting engagement and focus.

Learning Curve

Every software comes with its own learning curve. Players unfamiliar with the platform may find themselves struggling with the controls, detracting from their ability to engage with the narrative.

BEST PRACTICES FOR PROFESSIONAL GAME MASTERS

Master Your Tools

Before you introduce players to a new virtual platform, make sure you've mastered it yourself. Understand its capabilities, limitations, and quirks. Conduct test runs to smooth out potential hiccups.

Keep It Simple

Especially when you're starting out, less is often more. Use only the features that enhance storytelling and player engagement; ignore the rest until you're more comfortable with the software.

Session Zero Revisited

Consider having a technology-specific Session Zero where you introduce the platform to your players, allowing them to get comfortable with the controls and features in a low-stakes setting.

Be Prepared

Have contingency plans in place for technical glitches. Know how to quickly solve common issues and have a backup platform handy if needed.

Periodic Check-Ins

Regularly seek feedback from your players about their experience with the virtual tabletop. Adjust your use of the technology accordingly.

By taking the time to understand and master your chosen technology, you can ensure that it serves as an aid to storytelling rather than a distraction. After all, as a professional Game Master, your primary objective is to deliver a seamless and immersive experience, whether you're gathered around a physical table or connected through pixels and code.

IMPORTANT NOTICE: RULES FOR PROFESSIONAL GAME MASTERS ON ONLINE PLATFORMS

As a professional Game Master, it's essential to understand that not all online platforms share the same policies regarding paid games. Ignorance is not an excuse, and failing to adhere to a platform's guidelines could result in your game being delisted or even result in a ban from the platform altogether. Here are some things to consider:

Read The Terms Of Service

Before posting your paid game listing on any platform—Discord, D&D Beyond, Roll20, or others—thoroughly read their Terms of Service, focusing specifically on the rules regarding paid services. Some platforms may not allow the advertisement of paid games at all, while others might have restrictions or specific channels for such listings.

Revenue Sharing Or Platform Fees

Some platforms may require you to share a percentage of your earnings with them if you're using their service to host paid games. Be sure you're aware of any financial commitments you're making by listing your game on a specific platform.

Required Disclosures

Many platforms will require you to clearly and conspicuously disclose that your game is a paid or professional service. The specifics of how and where to disclose this information can vary by platform, so ensure you follow the guidelines precisely.

Community Guidelines

Beyond the Terms of Service, many platforms have community guidelines you'll need to follow. These guidelines can affect how and where you can promote your services and what content you can include in your listings.

Restricted Content

Each platform might have its own rules about what content is allowable. Some might have restrictions based on age, genre, or subject matter, while others might be more liberal. Always double-check to ensure your game's content aligns with the platform's guidelines.

Reporting And Review Systems

Be aware that platforms often have reporting and review systems in place. Consistently low reviews or frequent user reports could negatively impact your listing and potentially your standing on the platform.

Continual Updates

Policies can and do change. Make a habit of regularly reviewing the guidelines and terms of these platforms to ensure you remain in compliance.

Being a professional means not just excelling at game mastering but also at understanding and navigating the various logistical and legal landscapes of online platforms. Your credibility and long-term success depend on it.

EXTENDING PRIME TIME: THE INTERNATIONAL MARKET FOR PROFESSIONAL GMS

The "Prime Time" Phenomenon

Most tabletop RPGs, like prime-time television, happen in the evening when people are off work and ready to relax. This natural clustering creates a peak demand window but also means that game masters compete with each other for players during these "prime time" hours.

The World Is Your Playground

The internet has opened up an international market that allows you to extend your "prime time" well beyond local evening hours. By catering to different time zones, you can fill up your day with multiple sessions, accommodating players worldwide.

Early Birds And Night Owls

If you're an early riser, you could run a morning session for players in Western Australia, who would be enjoying their evening. Conversely, if you're a night owl, you could cater to European players who are just starting their day.

Cultural Sensitivity and Inclusivity

While the global reach of online platforms provides an excellent opportunity, it also necessitates a nuanced approach to cultural and language differences. Always treat international players with respect. Make an effort to understand accents and language nuances, and be patient with players who may be struggling with language barriers. Including international players can enrich the social fabric of the gaming experience, making it more diverse and engaging for everyone involved.

Language Proficiency As An Asset

Suppose you're fluent in languages other than English or have a deep understanding of another culture. In that case, you possess a unique selling point. You could specialize in running games for communities often overlooked in the RPG world, creating a niche market for yourself.

Final Thoughts

The opportunities in the international market are vast, but they require an informed and sensitive approach. By extending your "prime time" to accommodate different time zones, respecting cultural differences, and leveraging your language skills and cultural knowledge, you can differentiate yourself in an increasingly crowded market.

CHAPTER 9: MASTERING THE ART OF STORYTELLING —PERSONAL ARCS, MEDIA INSPIRATION, AND CLASSIC PLOTS

Narration is your bread and butter in the world of tabletop role-playing games. As a professional Game Master, your storytelling prowess elevates the game from a mere mechanical exercise to an emotional journey. One need not have majored in English Literature to perform this job, (although it helps!)

The purpose of this chapter is to encourage you to think about how your narrative skills will make your campaign deeply meaningful for every player. You will learn how to focus on character story arcs, employing time-tested plots from literary fiction, and how to augment your skills by drawing inspiration from various media.

PERSONALIZING CHARACTER ARCS

Integrate Backstories

The best way to create a personalized experience is to incorporate each player's backstory into the overarching campaign narrative. Imagine a player has created a character whose parents were killed by a corrupt noble. You may be planning on running a campaign in which a troupe of goblins are troubling a farming village. You could take the opportunity to insert clues leading the party to realize that the goblins are being paid by said noble in an effort to vacate the village and seize the abandoned farms for himself.

Individual Quests

Characters are often motivated by personal quests. Sometimes, these quests are evident from the character's backstory; other times, the quests are given to the characters as the narrative progresses. For instance, as a part of their back story, a druid who was raised as a member of a wolf pack may have vowed to one day find and punish the hunter who slew his family in their den. On the other hand, an aimless paladin deeply connected to their deity will find profound meaning in a quest given by the Abbot of the local monastery to recover a lost holy artifact.

Emotional Stakes

It is your job to create emotionally charged situations that require characters to make difficult decisions. The party's warrior must choose between saving his brother or holding closed a gate behind which an eager orc horde has assembled to sack the castle.

DRAWING INSPIRATION FROM OTHER MEDIA

Movies And Tv Shows

Epic cinematic moments often make for equally compelling tabletop scenarios. Take the final battle in "The Lord of the Rings" or the space opera elements from "Battlestar Galactica." Consider how you can adapt these set pieces or themes to fit your campaign.

Cinematic pacing, high-stakes conflicts, and visual motifs from movies can serve as excellent templates for your campaign. Think of how the tension builds in thriller films or how characters evolve in drama. Use these structural elements to guide your storytelling.

Comics And Graphic Novels

The visual storytelling in comics like "Sandman" or "Saga" can be a fantastic source for describing scenes, settings, or even character appearance. You can also take inspiration from their story arcs to craft unique quests.

Books And Novels

Novels and literature offer complex narratives and character development, inspiring intricate plots and deep emotional arcs. Think of how a saga like 'The Lord of the Rings' unfolds, offering individual story arcs within an epic quest.

Books are a treasure trove of storytelling elements, from classic literature to modern fantasy novels. Whether it's the intricate political intrigue of "Game of Thrones" or the hero's journey in "The Odyssey," books offer in-depth narratives and character development techniques you can adapt.

Video Games

The quest structure of RPG video games like "The Elder Scrolls" or "The Witcher" series can serve as a blueprint for your campaign. How these games incorporate character choices can inspire you to make your adventures more interactive.

Comics

Sequential storytelling in comics allows for episodic adventures that are still part of a larger arc. The medium is also ripe for inspiration regarding visual descriptions and action sequences.

MAKING CAMPAIGNS MEMORABLE

The heart of any memorable role-playing game campaign is its story. As a professional Game Master, your responsibility is to weave a compelling narrative that entertains and allows for deep emotional investment. Let's delve into techniques that can make your campaign resonate with each player by intricately tying it to their character's story arc.

Balancing Popularity And Authenticity

In a saturated marketplace where tabletop role-playing games are increasingly becoming the go-to source of entertainment, standing out is crucial. As a professional Game Master, you're competing with hundreds, if not thousands, of other talented individuals. The question then arises: Should you go for what's currently popular or carve out a unique niche for yourself?

The Trap Of Trend-Chasing

Chasing after what's popular may seem like the easiest route to quick success, but this approach has its pitfalls. If you're running campaigns solely based on their trending status, your passion and enthusiasm may wane. Players can sense when a Game Master is not invested in the narrative. That lack of enthusiasm can dampen the entire experience.

The Power Of Authenticity

On the flip side, creating a unique campaign based on what truly excites you has several benefits. First, your genuine passion for the campaign topic will shine through, creating a more engaging and immersive experience for your players. Second, an original and unique campaign allows you to carve out a niche market, targeting players specifically interested in what you wish to offer.

Striking A Balance

So, how do you reconcile these two approaches to create a campaign that stands out and resonates with your target audience? Here are some strategies:

Market Research: Research popular themes and elements that resonate with players. Tracking current offerings on popular sites will give you insights into what players seek.

Client Consultation: During Session Zero or preliminary discussions, ask your players what campaign themes, characters, and experiences they are interested in.

Personal Enthusiasm: Choose a campaign theme that you're genuinely excited about. You'll be spending much time in this world, so it's crucial that you enjoy it.

Innovative Twists: Even if you choose a popular theme, think of ways to add your unique spin, such as a novel setting, an unexpected plot twist, or unconventional characters.

Quality Over Quantity: It's better to offer fewer sessions that you're genuinely passionate about than to spread yourself thin by running multiple campaigns you have little interest in.

Pilot Sessions: Run a few sessions as a 'pilot' to gauge interest and get player feedback. These sessions will help you make necessary adjustments before fully launching the campaign.

Continuous Feedback: Keep an open communication channel with your players to ensure that the campaign meets their expectations while still being something you love.

By striking the right balance between what's popular and what you're genuinely passionate about, you can create compelling campaigns that stand out in the marketplace and bring you both personal and professional fulfillment. Remember, the most memorable campaigns are born when the Game Master's enthusiasm is as palpable as the roll of the dice.

INCORPORATING CHARACTER ARCS

Personal Quests

Offer each player a personal quest that ties into their character's backstory or personal goals. This individual mission should stretch out over multiple sessions, giving the player a long-term objective contributing to their emotional journey.

Foils And Rivals

Introduce NPCs that serve as foils or rivals to the characters. Placing these figures in the campaign allows players to explore different facets of their character's personality.

The Reckoning

Every character has strengths and weaknesses, virtues and vices. Use the story to force characters into situations where they must face their shortcomings or make moral choices that challenge their beliefs. These "reckoning moments" make for dramatic storytelling and profound character development.

BASIC PLOTS IN LITERARY FICTION

The Hero's Journey

The timeless structure of a hero venturing forth, facing challenges, and returning transformed can serve as the backbone of your campaign. Each player's character embarks on a personal hero's journey, aligning their arcs with the broader quest.

Tragedy

Not all stories have happy endings. Tragedies can serve as powerful emotional experiences that leave a lasting impression. Use this sparingly and with consent from your players.

While not every campaign should end in despair, incorporating elements of tragedy can add emotional depth. A tragic arc could involve a beloved NPC, providing players with a lesson or a cautionary tale.

Comedy

Comedy refers not to the modern sense of humor but to the classical plotlines in which characters find themselves in increasingly complicated situations, only for all the confusion to be resolved neatly at the end. These plotlines can provide a satisfying conclusion to complex in-game politics or love triangles.

Mystery

The literary plot of unraveling a secret or solving a crime can easily be the central theme of a campaign. Whether it's a murder mystery in a royal court or the enigmatic origins of an ancient artifact, the suspense can keep players deeply engaged.

The Quest

It is a time-honored trope where characters embark on a journey to achieve a goal. Along the way, they encounter various challenges that test their mettle. A grand quest drives the party to reach a powerful objective.

Overcoming The Monster

The party must defeat a potent antagonist that represents a great evil. The climax often involves a showdown between the characters and a penultimate monster. It's a classic PvM campaign that pits the players against a single, overwhelming threat (think Tarrasque!)

Rags To Riches

Use this arc to progress the characters from humble beginnings to grand conclusions, where the riches need not be material but could be skill acquisition, divine powers, or influential allies.

In this plot, characters start with humble beginnings and rise to achieve great things. Rag to Riches is effective for long-term campaigns where players can see visible growth in their characters' power and influence.

Rebirth

This plot centers around themes of renewal or transformation. Characters might be involved in a quest that allows them to change or grow significantly, often after a low point or 'dark night of the soul.'

APPLYING LITERARY PLOTS TO CHARACTER ARCS

You can align the broader campaign arc with the individual character arcs. For example, in a 'Quest' campaign, each character could have a personal quest that complements the main objective. In an 'Overcoming the Monster' campaign, players could face their own personal 'monster'—a literal creature or a metaphorical demon.

The role of a Game Master goes beyond merely facilitating a game; you're crafting an experience that has the potential for both fun and emotional depth. By thoughtfully incorporating character arcs and drawing inspiration from diverse forms of storytelling, you elevate your campaign from a mere game to a compelling narrative journey.

By skillfully blending these storytelling techniques, you make the campaign vividly memorable and deeply meaningful for each player. You're not merely providing a service; you're creating an emotionally resonant experience, enhancing personal connections, and enriching your skill set as a professional Game Master.

In the following chapters, we'll explore other pillars of becoming a professional Game Master—from managing your sessions effectively to building your brand. But never forget: the story is the soul of your campaign. And when you master storytelling, you captivate the hearts and minds of your players, creating a campaign they'll talk about for years to come.

CHAPTER 11: THE FOUR PILLARS—COMBAT, SOCIAL, EXPLORATION, AND BALANCE FOR A SATISFYING CAMPAIGN

As a professional Game Master, your campaign is not just a story to be told; it's an experience to be lived by your players. To that end, understanding the balance between combat, social interactions, and exploration—the three pillars of role-playing games—is essential. By deftly weaving these aspects together, you can offer a rich tapestry of experiences that speak to different player preferences and expectations.

COMBAT: MORE THAN JUST ROLLING DICE

Emotional Stakes

Combat shouldn't be a mechanical affair devoid of narrative significance. Each battle should offer something more: an emotional stake, a plot development, or a moral dilemma.

Tactical Depth

Different players enjoy different types of combat challenges. Some relish tactical complexity, while others prefer straightforward brawls. Tailor combat scenarios to provide a variety of challenges that cater to different tactical preferences.

SOCIAL INTERACTIONS: THE HEART OF ROLE-PLAYING

Character Development

In social settings, characters with certain skill sets may shine, grow, and develop. Whether complex negotiations with a warring faction or a heart-to-heart with an NPC, these interactions allow players to explore their characters' complexities.

Plot Advancement

Social interactions shouldn't be filler. They should advance the plot, provide important information, or contribute to character development.

EXPLORATION: A WORLD BEYOND THE BATTLEFIELD

Sense Of Wonder

A well-crafted world can be a character in its own right. Use descriptive language, atmospheric elements, and interactive features to make the environment come alive.

Puzzles And Mysteries

Exploration isn't just physical; it's also intellectual. Incorporate puzzles, riddles, and mysteries to challenge your players and provide opportunities for non-combat victories.

The Fourth Pillar: Balance

Some would say that the 4rth pillar is the narrative. I am going to point to Balance. Recognize that every campaign will have its unique blend of these pillars depending upon the choices you and your group have made. And hopefully you will have blended these into the perfect combination to serve your players and their stories!

A combat-heavy session might be punctuated by moments of quiet dialogue or environmental storytelling. Likewise, a socially focused campaign might feature combat that emphasizes the interpersonal dynamics between characters.

Recognizing that all players are different and seeking a unique blend of these elements will help you craft a satisfying campaign for everyone involved. The key is to keep the lines of communication open and to be flexible enough to adjust your storytelling approach to meet the evolving needs of your players.

In the coming chapters, we'll dive into the logistical aspects of running a professional campaign, including managing time, setting the mood, and creating an inclusive environment. But for now, keep these pillars in mind—they are the foundation upon which all memorable campaigns are built.

CHAPTER 12: ADVANCED NARRATIVE TECHNIQUES FOR THE PROFESSIONAL GAME MASTER

When players reminisce about their most memorable campaigns, they invariably recall not just the thrill of combat or the puzzle of a complex riddle but the stories that made their characters feel alive and part of a living, breathing world. As a professional Game Master, you have the opportunity to elevate your storytelling to an art form, enriching your campaigns and creating experiences your players will treasure for years to come. Here are some advanced narrative techniques to consider:

Subverting Expectations

While classical story arcs and traditional tropes can provide a comforting familiarity, a well-placed twist can make your campaign unforgettable. Subvert expectations by presenting familiar scenarios but with an unexpected outcome. Perhaps the seemingly evil witch is a misunderstood guardian of the forest, or maybe the feared dragon is more interested in poetry than plunder.

Flashbacks And Flashforwards

These tools aren't just for movies or novels; they can also add depth to your RPG. Flashbacks can provide crucial backstories at pivotal moments, increasing the emotional stakes. Flashforwards can give tantalizing glimpses of potential futures, making players more invested in avoiding or ensuring particular outcomes.

Parallel Storylines

Having two or more interconnected storylines running simultaneously can give players the sense that they're part of a larger world where actions have far-reaching consequences. This can be as simple as two groups of adventurers aiming for the same goal but from different starting points or as complex as parallel universes affecting each other.

Epistolary Elements

Incorporate letters, diary entries, or even full-fledged books within the game. These can serve as quests, clues, or mere world-building elements that enrich the player's experience. It can also allow you to present information in an engaging and interactive manner.

Foreshadowing And Planting Information

Subtly introduce elements that will become important later on, either through environmental clues, dialogue, or premonitions. Effective foreshadowing can make the final reveal both surprising and inevitable, increasing player satisfaction.

Inner Conflicts And Moral Dilemmas

The most gripping stories often involve internal battles as much as external ones. Moral dilemmas can make for compelling narratives and stimulate player discussion. By challenging players to make hard choices that don't have straightforward 'right' or 'wrong' answers, you add complexity to both the characters and the story.

Recurring Themes And Motifs

Whether it's a recurring symbol, phrase, or situation, these elements can add depth and cohesion to your story. For example, a recurring motif of doors—literal and metaphorical— could symbolize new opportunities or hidden dangers, adding thematic depth to the campaign.

The Unreliable Npc

Not all storytellers within your world should tell the truth. Incorporate NPCs with their own motives for lying or bending the truth, making your players second-guess their interactions and weigh the reliability of the information they receive.

The Player's Backstory

Integrate elements from your players' backstories into the main campaign. This makes the story more personal and rewards players for their creative efforts in character creation.

By incorporating these advanced narrative techniques, you can craft campaigns that entertain, captivate, and engage on a deeper level. The key to using these tools effectively is always keeping your players' engagement in mind and adapting your approach to fit their interests and expectations. In doing so, you elevate your storytelling from mere narration to a shared storytelling experience, making your mark as a truly professional Game Master.

It's Not Your Story!

As a professional Game Master, it's easy to fall into the trap of thinking that you're the sole creator of the narrative world your players inhabit. After all, you've spent countless hours constructing the campaign setting, plotting intricate story arcs, and breathing life into NPCs. But remember this: you are not the only storyteller at the table, nor are you the most important one.

Shared Storytelling

The true magic of tabletop RPGs lies in the collective storytelling experience. Your players are not just passive recipients of your narrative; they are active co-authors. Their characters' decisions, triumphs, and failures shape the story in unexpected and often enriching ways.

Player Agency: The Heart Of The Game

Remember that the player's agency in the narrative is sacred. Their characters' choices should have real consequences, which should never be invalidated by a pre-determined plot or ending you've constructed. Player agency makes RPGs interactive and collaborative; it's the 'game' in a 'role-playing game.'

The Ever-Changing Narrative

Be prepared and willing to alter your carefully laid plans. If the characters' choices take the story on a different course, embrace it. The narrative should be flexible enough to incorporate these twists and turns. Even if it derails your original vision, the resulting story is often far more meaningful and engaging because it's born from collective creativity.

Elevate Their Stories

If a player's backstory or character arc can be incorporated or highlighted, do so—even if it means reshuffling your narrative or modifying your plans. The best stories often emerge from synthesizing everyone's contributions, including your players' often surprising and delightful input.

In sum, while you are a storyteller, the most captivating and rewarding narratives emerge when you share that role with your players. Their contributions—expected or not—will make your campaigns genuinely unforgettable. So step back, guide rather than dictate, and let the collective storytelling unfold.

CHAPTER 13: NAVIGATING SENSITIVE AND PROBLEMATIC ELEMENTS IN TABLETOP RPGS

As a professional Game Master, you hold a unique position of power at the gaming table: you set the tone, control the narrative, and guide the players through a world of your making. With that power comes the responsibility to create an inclusive and respectful environment, which means being mindful of potentially harmful or triggering elements that have historically been part of tabletop role-playing games.

Problematic Tropes Of The Past

Tabletop RPGs, like any other form of media, are a product of their times. That means they sometimes reflect the biases, prejudices, and stereotypes of the eras in which they were created. Early editions of many RPGs, not limited to Dungeons and Dragons, have been criticized for perpetuating racist, sexist, or otherwise harmful stereotypes—whether through the presentation of certain races as inherently evil or through overly sexualized depictions of female characters.

Acknowledging The Issue

The first step in addressing these problems is acknowledging them. Ignoring or dismissing the problematic elements in older editions won't make them go away, and it can also harm players affected by these issues.

AVOIDING STEREOTYPES

Race And Culture In Rpgs

The concept of "race" in many fantasy RPGs can often perpetuate harmful stereotypes if not handled carefully. Aim for depth and complexity rather than leaning on one-dimensional portrayals when designing NPCs or cultures. Remember that no race or culture should be universally good or evil, smart or stupid, noble or treacherous.

Gender And Sexuality

Avoid relying on gender stereotypes or roles when constructing your campaigns. The days when all fighters were men and all healers were women should be long behind us. Be aware of how your game can support various gender identities and expressions.

Disabilities

Rather than using disabilities to limit characters or make them objects of pity, try to present them in a respectful and inclusive way. There are many ways to be a hero, and physical or mental disabilities shouldn't prevent a character from being competent and valuable.

Consent And Safety Mechanisms

Before diving into themes that could be triggering or controversial, such as violence, discrimination, or mental illness, make sure you have explicit consent from all players. Use safety tools like lines and veils or the X-card system to give players an out if they feel uncomfortable (see Chapter 5 for more on safety tools).

Being An Ally At The Table

As a professional Game Master, your role extends beyond just running the game—you're also a moderator and, in some ways, a community leader. Suppose you witness harmful stereotypes perpetuated at your table. In that case, it's your job to step in and correct the behavior, always aiming for education over confrontation.

The Importance Of Inclusion

As a professional Game Master, your primary goal is to create an immersive and enjoyable experience for all your players. Inclusivity should be an integral part of that experience. An inclusive table isn't just a "nice to have"—it's necessary to broaden your client base and enrich your storytelling.

Preferred Pronouns And Respecting Identity

Begin each new session or campaign with a brief discussion about preferred pronouns. Not only does this set the tone for an inclusive table, but it also shows that you're a respectful and professional Game Master. Use and respect the pronouns your players provide for them and their characters.

Being Accommodating

Be prepared to make accommodations to ensure everyone feels comfortable and included. For players with disabilities, this might mean ensuring physical accessibility to the play area or offering assistive technologies for online sessions. It could also involve providing campaign materials in accessible formats.

Harmful Stereotypes And Language

As the Game Master, you control the narrative and how cultures, characters, and situations are portrayed. Educate yourself about harmful stereotypes, particularly racial and cultural caricatures, and actively work to exclude these from your game. The same applies to language; avoid using ableist or discriminatory speech in and out of character. If a player is concerned about something in your game, listen and be willing to adjust.

The Learning Curve

While you might be a seasoned Game Master, there's always more to learn regarding inclusivity. This could mean attending seminars, taking online courses, or simply staying abreast of conversations about diversity and inclusion in the gaming community. Never stop learning.

Creating A Safe Space

Include content warnings where applicable and use tools like the X-card or established safe words to give players an out if they're uncomfortable. Open lines of communication with your players to ensure everyone feels safe and heard. After all, role-playing can evoke strong emotional reactions, and players must have the space to express any discomfort they may feel.

Celebrating Diversity

An inclusive game is a better game, full of rich narratives, complex characters, and a table that reflects the diversity of our world. It is important to recognize the unique perspective that every player brings to the gaming table. Encourage characters from different backgrounds and experiences, as these details can add depth and realism to your storytelling.

Conclusion

Inclusivity is not a one-time action but an ongoing commitment. Constantly strive to make your table as open and welcoming as possible. Your game will be better for it, and you'll find that the world you create becomes all the richer when a diverse cast of characters and players inhabits it.

By being aware of these issues and taking proactive steps to make your games more inclusive, you're contributing to a more welcoming and respectful RPG community. After all, the ultimate goal of any game is for everyone at the table to have fun, and that's much easier to achieve when everyone feels seen, respected, and safe.

THE HALF-ORC INTELLIGENCE CAP - A PROBLEMATIC LEGACY

When discussing the historical issues within tabletop role-playing games, one standout example is the intelligence maximum applied to Half-Orc characters in original D&D editions. This rule stipulated that Half-Orcs could only reach a certain level of intelligence, limiting their potential in ways other races were not subjected to.

Reflecting Or Reinforcing Stereotypes?

Whether intentionally or not, this limitation mirrored certain stereotypes and prejudices of the era, essentially encoding them into the game's mechanics. It reinforced the notion that some races were innately "less intelligent" and sent a subliminal message to players that such distinctions were natural and unchangeable. This had deeply troubling implications in a game that often involves killing or subjugating creatures based on their racial alignment.

Modern Shifts: Equality And Inclusivity

Fast forward to today, and you'll find a much different landscape in the world of tabletop role-playing. Modern editions of games like Dungeons & Dragons have overwhelmingly rejected such racially-based limitations. In today's games, a Half-Orc can be as intelligent, wise, or charismatic as any other character. This reflects a broader cultural shift within the gaming community, emphasizing inclusivity, equality, and the decoupling of abilities from racial or ethnic backgrounds.

In other words, if you want your Half-Orc Wizard to have the highest Intelligence score in the campaign, nothing is stopping you. Today's tabletop RPGs strive to be a canvas where everyone can tell their stories, free from the constraints of outdated and harmful ideologies.

It's important for all players—and particularly professional Game Masters committed to creating inclusive environments —to be aware of this history, not to shame the past, but to better understand the present and guide our steps into a more equitable future.

CHAPTER 14: DEALING WITH THE PROBLEM PLAYER - "WHEN ONE PERSON'S NOT HAVING FUN, NOBODY IS HAVING FUN"

Being a professional Game Master means you're in a position not just to entertain and engage but also to mediate and manage social dynamics. Inevitably, you'll encounter a "problem player"—someone whose behavior negatively impacts the game for everyone else. As Matt Colville aptly puts it, "When one person's not having fun, nobody is having fun."

Identifying The Problem Player

Problem players come in various forms: the rule-breaker, the spotlight hogger, the aggressor, the constant skeptic, and many more. What they all have in common is that their actions disrupt the flow of the game and detract from the enjoyment of others. You'll often find that other players begin to dread sessions, or the enthusiasm that once permeated your group diminishes. When that happens, you know you have a situation that needs to be addressed.

ADDRESSING PROBLEMS AT THE TABLE

Gentle Reminders

Sometimes, a simple "Hey, let's keep it civil" or "Remember, it's a cooperative game" will suffice. A gentle reminder during gameplay can steer a wayward player back on course without halting the game.

Pausing For A Moment

For more severe disruptions, it might be necessary to pause the game momentarily. Address the issue openly but diplomatically, taking care to avoid blaming or shaming. Say something like, "I think we're getting off track here; let's refocus."

The One-On-One Conversation

If the disruptive behavior continues, it may be time for a private, one-on-one conversation with the problem player. Discuss your observations and explain how their actions affect the game for everyone else. Use "I" statements to avoid making the player defensive, for instance: "I've noticed that the tone becomes tense when you aggressively argue about rules."

The Last Resort: Asking A Player To Leave

The phrase "Maybe you should find some other people to play with," also attributed to Matt Colville, is a last-resort option but always an option nonetheless. Asking a player to leave is always challenging. Still, suppose someone is consistently ruining the experience for others and has yet to respond to multiple interventions. In that case, it may be the best course of action for the health of the group. The key here is to be direct but compassionate. State clearly why it's not working out, and make it about the dynamics of the group rather than personal failings.

Conclusion

As a professional Game Master, your primary duty is to create an enjoyable experience for all your players. That sometimes means making tough calls to preserve the integrity of the group. Preparing for these challenging moments and handling them with sensitivity and assertiveness can make all the difference. Remember, your objective is to create an environment where everyone can have fun—and sometimes, that might mean making difficult decisions to ensure the collective good.

CHAPTER 15: BUSINESS CONSIDERATIONS FOR THE PROFESSIONAL GAME MASTER

So, you've mastered the art of storytelling, honed your interpersonal skills, and are ready to take your passion for role-playing games to a professional level. Before you do, there are several business considerations you'll need to keep in mind to ensure that your endeavor is not only fulfilling but also financially viable.

Taxes And Financial Structures

As a professional Game Master, you'll be generating income, meaning you'll need to pay taxes. In many jurisdictions, freelance income is subject to self-employment tax. There are several ways to manage this, and one option to consider is setting up a Limited Liability Company (LLC) for your business. An LLC can offer legal protection and potential tax benefits.

Note: This manual is not a substitute for professional financial advice. You should always consult with your own qualified financial advisor to discuss your specific needs and circumstances.

EXPENSES TO KEEP IN MIND

Online Subscriptions

Platforms like Roll20 and Dndbeyond offer various subscription levels that provide additional features that can significantly enhance your game sessions. While not strictly necessary, these subscriptions can provide valuable tools that make your life easier and improve the player experience.

Patreon And Other Content

Some GMs subscribe to Patreons to access unique maps, quests, and other resources. These assets can add a layer of polish to your campaigns and help you stand out from the crowd.

Books And Digital Copies

As a GM, you'll need multiple formats of the same resource —rulebooks, campaign guides, or adventure modules. Whether operating online or in person, you'll need physical books and digital copies to maximize your effectiveness and adaptability. And yes, you'll usually have to buy them separately.

Pricing Your Services

Determining how much to charge for your services can be tricky. Start by researching what other GMs are charging on various platforms. Over the past few years, GM fees have been slowly rising, reflecting both the increasing demand for GM services and the ever-growing array of tools and resources available.

Resist The Urge To Undercut

While it may be tempting to lower your prices to attract more players, this can often backfire and result in a "race to the bottom," devaluing not just your work but all professional GMs. Instead of cutting your prices, focus on enhancing your service and recruiting players willing to pay for the quality experience you offer.

Conclusion

Turning your passion for game mastering into a career is a rewarding but complex endeavor that involves various financial and business considerations. From taxes and potential LLCs to expenses and pricing strategies, you must plan carefully to turn your professional GMing venture into a long-term success. Always remember that this is a real business, deserving of the same level of consideration and planning as any other.

CHAPTER 16: KNOW YOUR MATERIAL! - BRINGING WORLDS TO LIFE

Being a professional Game Master is akin to being a director, set designer, scriptwriter, and actor all rolled into one. One of your most crucial roles is that of the world-builder. Whether working with a published campaign setting or your own "homebrew" world, a deep and detailed understanding of the material is essential for creating an immersive and engaging experience.

Homebrew vs. Published Worlds

Homebrew Worlds

Find any good GM, and you will hear about their Homebrew. Everyone has one, and believe it is the very best world ever! That abundance of enthusiasm is necessary for the Game Master who wishing to create your own world from scratch. World Building can be immensely rewarding. You have the freedom to shape geography, culture, history, and more. However, this freedom comes with the responsibility of creating a coherent, believable world. You must understand your setting inside and out, from the grand sweep of empires to the minute details of a local tavern.

Published Worlds

Conversely, running a game in a well-known world like Faerûn or Golarion brings its own set of challenges. These settings come with extensive lore that many players are deeply familiar with, thanks to countless novels, video games, and published adventures. In these cases, your preparation should involve a deep dive into existing material to ensure you meet or exceed your players' expectations.

The Weight Of Player Expectations

For settings that have been extensively developed, players will often come with expectations built up by their experiences with novels, video games, or other media. They have dreamed of adventuring in these worlds, and it's your job to make that dream a reality. Failure to capture the essence of the world can result in an unsatisfying game, no matter how good you are at other aspects of game mastering.

Blend Of Both

Perhaps the best way to build and maintain a world is by borrowing from the published worlds, and then diverting into your own version of that world. This allows you to build on well established lore and histories but eventually you will be building a unique blend which suits you and your players the best. So, just because some old module refers to all Trolls as stupid and carnivorous, you can feel free to create a vegan troll who writed poetry, if you wish and most importantly, if that will delight your players.

Shared World-Building Through Character Backstories

While your preparation and mastery of the world's lore are essential, world-building is not a task you must undertake alone. Encourage players to develop detailed backstories for their characters. These backstories can inform the world itself, adding new cities, cultures, and conflicts you may not have conceived independently.

Incorporate these elements into your campaign, making them as much a part of the world as any published lore. This makes the setting richer and increases player investment; after all, it's now a world that they have helped to create.

Conclusion

The setting is more than just a backdrop for the campaign; it's a character in its own right, interacting with the players and shaping the story. The better you know your material, the more vibrant and engaging your world will be. So delve deep into the lore, whether you're creating it yourself or drawing on decades of published material. Your expertise will bring the world to life, creating an unforgettable experience for your players.

CHAPTER 17: BUILDING A PLAYER COMMUNITY: TOOLS AND TECHNIQUES

Pro vs. Friends - The Game Master Experience

Whether a casual game among friends or a professionally run campaign, the essence of tabletop role-playing games remains the same: collaborative storytelling, however, the role and responsibilities of the Game Master (GM) can differ significantly depending on the context. Let's explore the differences between running a game for your friends, and running a game as a professional experience.

With Friends: A Casual Setting

When you're the GM in a casual, friend-based setting, the game is often a collaborative endeavor in a different sense. Here, the GM and players are usually on equal footing, sharing the responsibility for creating a fun and engaging experience. The rules might be bent more often, and there's generally more room for improvisation.

As A Professional: A Client-Centric Approach

In contrast, a professional GM has different responsibilities. Here, the players are clients, so their unique needs and desires take center stage. You can be friends with your clients, but your primary goal is to offer the highest-quality gaming experience possible.

Client Needs And Preferences

Understanding your clients' needs goes beyond knowing the game mechanics and the campaign setting. It means understanding what each player seeks in the game—complex puzzles, intricate role-playing opportunities, or epic combat—and structuring the game to meet those needs. It may also mean adhering strictly to rules and published lore to maintain a consistent, high-quality experience.

Your Desires Take A Back Seat

As a professional GM, your preferences for the game—like wanting to explore a particular story arc or incorporate a cool new mechanic—take a back seat to client satisfaction. This doesn't mean you can't enjoy yourself or put your unique spin on the campaign. Still, your priority is to create an experience tailored to your players.

The core difference between GMing for friends and clients boils down to your focus and responsibilities. In a professional setting, you are a service provider aiming to meet and exceed your clients' expectations. This requires a different approach but offers its own set of personal and financial rewards.

Showing Gratitude: Strengthening Player-Gm Relationships

Building a strong relationship with your players is not merely a nice to have; it's an essential aspect of being a successful professional Game Master. Players who feel valued and appreciated are likelier to return for future campaigns, recommend your services, and contribute positively to the game environment. Gratitude is the cornerstone of this relationship. So, how can you authentically express gratitude and recognition to your players?

In-Game Recognition

Acknowledging Achievements: During a session, recognize exceptional role-playing, strategic thinking, or teamwork. A simple "Well done!" can go a long way.

Lore Incorporation: Integrate a character's backstory, achievements, or unique skills into the campaign's lore. For instance, a bard might compose a song about the heroic deeds of a player's character.

Character-Specific Quests: Develop subplots or quests highlighting a character's strengths, backstory, or objectives. This shows that you're paying attention to each player's individual narrative.

Session Recaps: Begin each session with a recap that not only refreshes the main plot points but also highlights the standout moments for characters in the last session.

Out-Of-Game Appreciation

Personal Thank-You Messages: After a session, a quick thank-you message expressing your appreciation for their engagement can make a big impact.

Feedback Conversations: Show you value their input by asking for feedback and implementing suggestions where appropriate.

Social Media Shoutouts: With player consent, sharing memorable moments or standout performances on social media can be a great way to show appreciation.

Player Spotlights: Some GMs like to do a 'Player of the Month' spotlight featuring an interview with the player about their character, their best moments in the campaign, and their approach to role-playing.

Gifts and Giveaways: Small gifts, like custom artwork of their characters or giving away sourcebooks or miniatures, can serve as tangible tokens of your appreciation. Make sure this is balanced and fair to all players.

The Importance Of Genuine Affection

Remember, genuine affection and respect for your players is the key to all this. It's not about flattery or empty gestures; it's about recognizing the collaborative nature of role-playing games and appreciating everyone's contribution to the shared storytelling experience.

Open And Clear Communication

Maintain open lines of communication with your players. This is not just beneficial for you as a Game Master in terms of feedback; it also reinforces to the players that their opinions and feelings matter to you.

By applying these strategies, you're not just thanking your players but building a community. You're creating an environment where players feel valued and appreciated, which enriches the current campaign and lays the groundwork for fulfilling and successful future campaigns. And in doing so, you're not just a professional Game Master; you're a pivotal part of each player's journey in the world of role-playing.

DAVID CUSACK

LEVERAGING DISCORD AND BEYOND

As a professional Game Master, your success isn't solely determined by how well you can create an engaging story or how intricately you've mapped out your campaign world. A critical aspect of your role is also building a player community. This loyal audience not only participates in your games but also enriches the experience for everyone involved. In today's digital age, tools like Discord have become indispensable for community-building. In this chapter, we'll explore how you can effectively use these platforms to cultivate a vibrant, engaged player community.

Discord: The Game Master's Best Friend

Discord has emerged as a powerful tool for the gaming community, RPGs included. Beyond just a text and voice chat platform, Discord offers a plethora of features that can benefit you as a professional Game Master:

Channels: Organize discussions through multiple text channels, each dedicated to different aspects like general chat, campaign lore, or rule clarifications.

Voice Rooms: Conduct sessions in dedicated voice rooms and set permissions so only selected members can join.

Bots: Utilize bots for role assignments, rule references, or even dice rolls.

File Sharing: Share important documents, maps, or images directly within the app.

Community Building: Use Discord to keep players engaged between sessions with discussions, puzzles, or lore drops.

Setting Up Your Discord Server

Creating a Discord server for your gaming community can be as simple or complex as you want it to be. Here are some suggestions:

Welcome Channel: Have an intro channel where new members can learn about the community rules and how to get involved.

Session Announcements: Make a channel solely for important dates, session summaries, and announcements to keep everyone in the loop.

Character Lore: Encourage players to share their characters' backstories, diaries, or art.

Off-Topic Channels: Give players room to socialize and discuss other interests, helping them form bonds outside of the game.

Feedback and Suggestions: Keep a channel for constructive criticism and ideas for improving the campaign.

Leveraging Discord For Networking And Growth

Your Discord server can be a hub for not only current players but also prospective ones. Consider the following:

Public vs. Private Channels: Keep some channels public to attract new members who can see the vibrancy of your community before deciding to join a campaign.

Showcase Highlights: Share epic moments, great role-playing instances, or artwork to give a taste of what your campaigns can offer.

Affiliations and Partnerships: Partner with other Game Masters or gaming communities to mutually promote each other.

Beyond Discord: Social Media And Streaming

Discord can be a nucleus, but remember the power of other platforms like Twitter, Twitch, or YouTube. Sharing content or streaming sessions can bring in a wider audience and add another revenue stream.

Caveats And Moderation

While Discord is a powerful tool, it's essential to maintain a safe and respectful environment. Set clear rules, utilize a Code of Conduct, and consider appointing moderators from your trusted player base.

Conclusion

Discord provides an incredible community-building platform that goes beyond any single campaign's immediate needs. As a professional Game Master, it's a tool you should leverage not just as a chat app but as a comprehensive hub for your player community. Combined with your skills and the other platforms at your disposal, you can build an engaged, thriving community that will enrich your games and prove rewarding on a personal level.

CHAPTER 18:
THE FINAL ACT
- CONCLUDING
THE CAMPAIGN
WITH GRACE

All good stories must come to an end, and so must your campaigns. The finale is more than just the conclusion of a plot; it's the culmination of weeks, months, or even years of shared storytelling. As a professional Game Master, how you conclude the campaign is just as critical as how you start it. This chapter will guide you through plotting a suitable sendoff for your characters and saying goodbye to your players while laying the groundwork for future adventures.

Crafting A Satisfying Conclusion

Every campaign has its unique tone, objectives, and narrative arcs; your ending should honor that uniqueness. Whether it's an epic battle against an ancient evil or fulfilling a long-sought quest, ensure that the finale resolves the plot and character arcs you've spent so much time building.

Fulfill Character Arcs: Tailor individual epilogues for each character that see them achieving personal goals or changing in significant ways.

Pay-Off Plot Hooks: Now is the time to tie up loose ends and resolve subplots, rewarding your players for their involvement and attentiveness.

Narrative Closure: Use vivid descriptions and emotionally charged narration to make the ending memorable. This is your last chance to evoke strong emotions, so make it count.

Treasures and Rewards: Besides in-game loot or magical items, consider real-life mementos like custom artwork of their characters or a well-crafted summary of their heroics as a keepsake.

Saying Goodbye To Players And Characters

The end of a campaign often comes with a sense of loss. Still, it's also an opportunity for reflection and celebration.

Debriefing Session: After the finale, hold a session where players can share their thoughts and feelings about the campaign. Discuss highs, lows, and memorable moments.

Thank You Notes: A personalized note thanking each player for contributing can go a long way.

Social Media Shoutouts: Recognize your players publicly if they're comfortable with it, celebrating your shared storytelling journey.

Reunion Sessions: These are one-off sessions held weeks or months after the campaign's end, allowing characters to reunite and players to catch up. This can be both nostalgic and fulfilling.

Beyond 'The End'

Remember, the conclusion of one tale can be the prologue to

another adventure. Use the ending to plant seeds for potential future campaigns, either as cliffhangers or as open questions that could form the basis of a new story.

Spin-offs: Side characters or unresolved plot elements can be the focus of a spin-off campaign.

Sequels: If the characters and world have more stories to tell, don't hesitate to plan a sequel.

One-Shots: These can serve as a testbed for new campaign ideas or a way to continue the story in a less time-consuming format.

Conclusion

Your role as a professional Game Master doesn't end when the story does. How you conclude a campaign will leave a lasting impression on your players and could decide whether they join you on future adventures. The end is a new beginning, so make it a memorable one. By doing so, you honor the story you've all created and enrich the ongoing narrative of each player's role-playing experience.

CHAPTER 19: CORPORATE GIGS - BRINGING TABLETOP RPGS INTO THE BOARDROOM

As a professional Game Master, you may find yourself in unique settings that differ from the casual gaming table. One such opportunity is facilitating a one-shot session in a corporate environment, often intended for team-building or training activities. Here's how you can adapt your approach to fit the corporate culture while ensuring everyone has a memorable experience.

Understand The Client's Needs

Before you roll the dice, discuss the session's objectives with the corporate client. Are they looking for team-building, problem-solving exercises, or a fun break from a long conference? Knowing the purpose will guide you in tailoring the experience.

SIMPLIFY, SIMPLIFY, SIMPLIFY!

Character Sheets

Corporate sessions will present you with players who are new to tabletop RPGs or are even entirely unfamiliar with the concept. A simplified character sheet highlighting the essential aspects can go a long way.

Pre-Generated Characters

Always come prepared with a roster of pre-generated characters that serve different roles so that players can jump right into the action without getting bogged down by the character-creation process.

Rules And Mechanics

Limit the use of complex rules and mechanics. In a corporate setting, the focus is usually on achieving a particular goal rather than delving into the nuances of the game system.

Time Management Is Key

Corporate clients are often on a tight schedule. Make sure your session fits within the allocated time slot without running over.

Prepare a storyline that can be comfortably completed within this timeframe, and always keep an eye on the clock.

Engagement Over Role-Playing

In a typical RPG session, role-playing is a significant aspect. However, in a corporate setting, focus more on keeping every player engaged through:

Strategy: Incorporate scenarios that require collective decision-making.

Puzzles: Utilize puzzles that need various skill sets to solve, emphasizing the importance of diverse talents within a team.

Clear Goals: The objectives should be straightforward and communicated clearly at the beginning of the session and repeated to avoid any confusion.

Recap And Debrief

After the session, take a few moments to recap the storyline and the choices made by the players, highlighting the team-building or training goals of the session. Depending on the client's needs, you may provide a brief written summary highlighting these aspects.

In Summary

Corporate gigs offer an exciting avenue for professional Game Masters to showcase the versatility and potential of tabletop RPGs as tools for more than just entertainment. However, the corporate setting also requires a shift in approach. By focusing on simplified gameplay, clear objectives, and maximum engagement, you can deliver a rewarding experience that meets the unique needs of your corporate clients.

CHAPTER 20: THE EMERGENCE OF THERAPEUTIC GAME MASTERS

The landscape of professional game mastering is ever-evolving, and one of the most intriguing developments is the rise of Therapeutic Game Masters. This specialized field merges the therapeutic milieu with the structure and storytelling of tabletop RPGs, offering unique therapeutic benefits to various groups, including those in group therapy and students with Educational Intervention Plans (EIPs).

Becoming A Certified Therapeutic Game Master

While anyone with the skills and inclination can become a Game Master, stepping into the realm of therapy requires additional training and certification. The idea is to equip the professional Game Master with the skills to effectively use tabletop RPGs as a therapeutic tool. This certification is typically offered through accredited programs that teach game masters therapeutic communication skills, ethical guidelines, and evidence-based interventions specific to this modality.

ADVANTAGES FOR THE TYPICAL CLIENT IN GROUP THERAPY

Enhanced Social Skills

Through the process of cooperative gameplay and narrative storytelling, clients can develop better communication and social skills. The structured environment of a tabletop RPG allows individuals to practice interactions in a controlled setting.

Emotional Regulation

In role-playing scenarios, individuals can face challenges, make decisions, and experience 'consequences' in a safe space. This can help teach emotional regulation and coping skills.

Self-Reflection

Role-playing can be a mirror reflecting deeper emotional and psychological issues. It provides a platform to explore these concerns under the guidance of a therapeutic game master.

Benefits for Students with EIPs

Goal-Oriented Tasks

Therapeutic tabletop RPGs can be customized to focus on specific learning outcomes or social goals that align with a student's EIP.

Collaborative Learning

Tabletop RPGs are naturally collaborative. For students struggling with social skills or team-based activities, this offers a chance to improve in these areas in a fun, less intimidating setting.

Enhanced Engagement

Tabletop RPGs can capture the imagination in ways that traditional therapeutic or educational methods might not. This increased engagement can lead to better outcomes.

Safely Explore Challenges

For students with EIPs, you can tailor the experience to present them with challenges similar to those they face in the educational environment, allowing them to develop coping strategies in a low-risk setting.

Extending Your Services

Being a certified Therapeutic Game Master opens new avenues of opportunity, from working in educational institutions to offering specialized group therapy sessions. It's a way to expand your skill set, providing value-added services that go beyond entertainment to bring meaningful change in the lives of your players.

In Summary

The role of a Therapeutic Game Master is rewarding and multi-faceted, offering psychological and educational benefits to diverse groups of individuals. By undergoing specialized training, a professional game master can make a significant impact while broadening their scope of services. Whether you're working with clients in a therapeutic setting or students with unique educational needs, the skills you gain as a Therapeutic Game Master will enhance your ability to bring about meaningful, lasting change.

CHAPTER 21: MASTERING CONVENTIONS – A GUIDE FOR THE PROFESSIONAL GAME MASTER

Conventions offer a unique playground for professional game masters, full of opportunities to showcase your talent, network with like-minded individuals, and even earn a decent income. Whether you're interested in representing a company or going solo, the convention experience is quite different from your standard, home-based sessions. Here's how to navigate it successfully.

Company Affiliation vs. Independent GMing

Representing A Company

Many tabletop RPG companies hire experienced game masters

to showcase their games at conventions. You'll be given a script to follow, marketing materials, and perhaps some swag to hand out to players. The company usually covers your ticket and sometimes even travel and lodging. However, you'll likely be working long hours with little room for personal exploration of the convention.

Independent Gming

If you go solo, you can run whatever game you like, be it a known system or your homebrew. You're responsible for all costs, including ticket, travel, and lodging. However, you can set your schedule and enjoy the convention at your own pace.

FEE STRUCTURES AT CONVENTIONS

Paid Events

Many conventions, like Gen Con, offer a platform where you can charge for your sessions. Fees can range from $2-4 per hour per player for less well-known GMs to $10-15 per hour per player for established professionals. Consider your reputation and expertise when setting your price.

Free Events

Some conventions offer free events as a way to attract more attendees. While you won't earn directly from these, you can gain exposure, collect contacts for future paid games, and sometimes even receive tips.

Sponsored Tables

Some game masters run events on behalf of a sponsor, usually a gaming company or retailer. They might provide you with free merchandise or a stipend in exchange for showcasing their products.

WHAT TO KEEP
IN MIND

Plan For The Unknown

Convention players can vary widely in age, experience level, and expectations. Be prepared to adapt your style to fit the group.

Timing is Crucial

Conventions operate on a tight schedule. Make sure your adventure fits within the allotted time. Remember, some players may have back-to-back events to attend.

Networking

Bring your business cards and get ready to network. This is your chance to make connections that can lead to future opportunities.

Player Experience

Conventions are hectic, but your table is an oasis. Strive to offer the best experience possible to stand out and make a lasting impression.

Wrapping Up

Conventions offer a unique opportunity to shine as a

professional game master. Whether representing a company or flying solo, the experience can be both rewarding and challenging. Understand the landscape, prepare diligently, and make your table unforgettable.

CHAPTER 22: THE EVER-EXPANDING UNIVERSE OF RESOURCES AND CONTINUOUS LEARNING

A Multitude Of Sources

In today's digital age, the variety of resources available to a professional Game Master is vast and ever-growing. From official rulebooks, expansions, and modules to fan-made content, podcasts, and YouTube series, you have a treasure trove of materials to deepen your understanding of your chosen game system, campaign, or setting. Utilizing various sources can elevate your games, providing a richer and more nuanced experience for your players.

Expanding The Lore

Supplementary materials like novels, comics, or lore-specific websites can offer a more detailed understanding of a particular setting. This is especially useful if you're running a campaign set in a well-established universe, where players may have expectations for a certain level of authenticity and depth.

Mechanics And House Rules

Podcasts, YouTube tutorials, and online forums are excellent resources for understanding game mechanics, potential house rules, and creative ways to deal with challenges that may arise during gameplay. Learning from others' experiences can save time and make your sessions more engaging.

The Journey To Mastery Is Never-Ending

Even after you've run countless sessions and consider yourself an experienced GM, there's always room for improvement. Game mechanics evolve, new storytelling techniques emerge, and player preferences change. The most successful professional GMs continually seek to improve their craft.

ENGAGE IN THE COMMUNITY

Online Forums And Social Media

Places like Reddit, dedicated Discord servers, and specialized Facebook groups offer a platform to interact with a community of like-minded individuals. You can share your experiences, learn from others, and keep up with the latest trends and news in the tabletop RPG world.

Conventions And Webinars

While online resources are invaluable, nothing beats the experience of attending GM-specific panels at conventions or participating in webinars. These experiences offer a deep dive into specialized topics and provide an opportunity to network with industry professionals.

Final Thoughts

Continuous improvement is a cornerstone of professionalism in any field, and game mastering is no different. Keeping abreast of the latest innovations, engaging with the community, and utilizing a wide array of resources is critical for delivering the best experience to your players. In a realm as dynamic and expansive as tabletop RPGs, lifelong learning is not just an advantage—it's a necessity.

CHAPTER 23: HARNESSING AI FOR MASTERFUL GAME ENHANCEMENT

In the realm of tabletop role-playing games the Game Master is the architect of worlds, the voice of characters, and the arbiter of rules—a storyteller and referee rolled into one. With the advent of artificial intelligence (AI), we now stand at the threshold of a new era, where the digital and the imagined seamlessly intertwine to elevate the art of game management to unprecedented heights. This chapter delves into the symbiotic relationship between GMs and AI, exploring how AI can act as both a muse and a toolset, enhancing the depth and breadth of interactive storytelling.

AI in gaming is not a new concept; however, its application in tabletop RPGs like Dungeons and Dragons has only recently begun to be fully realized. From creating richly detailed maps to populating worlds with dynamic non-player characters AI opens up a vast landscape of possibilities that can be tailored to the unique style of any GM. The potential benefits are manifold —AI can save time, inspire creativity, and provide on-the-spot assistance, allowing GMs to focus more on engaging their players and less on the minutiae of game mechanics and content generation.

This chapter is not about replacing the GM's role with algorithms; instead, it's about enhancing the human touch with digital efficiency. It is a guide for professional game masters to leverage AI as a powerful ally in crafting compelling narratives, creating immersive worlds, and managing the complex logistics of a gaming session. Whether you're a seasoned GM looking to incorporate cutting-edge tools into your repertoire or a newcomer eager to streamline your prep work, this chapter will provide insights into how AI can enrich your gaming sessions.

As we venture into the practical applications of AI for the professional GM, it is with the aim of keeping the spirit of tabletop RPGs alive: fostering creativity, camaraderie, and the thrill of adventure that brings players together around the table. With AI as your steadfast companion, the possibilities are as limitless as your imagination. Let's embark on this journey to discover how the fusion of technology and creativity can create a more vivid and engaging role-playing experience for everyone at the table.

Artificial intelligence (AI) has been a transformative force in the landscape of gaming, evolving from simple algorithmic opponents to complex systems capable of learning, adapting, and creating. In gaming, AI has traditionally been used to drive the behavior of non-player characters, creating challenges and interactions that feel natural and engaging to the player. However, its role has expanded far beyond these early applications.

In video games, AI has been responsible for revolutionizing gameplay, leading to opponents that can strategize, adapt to player behavior, and even exhibit learning behavior over the course of a game. Procedural generation, powered by AI, allows for the creation of vast, explorable worlds that offer a unique experience with every playthrough. Additionally, AI has enabled personalized gaming experiences through dynamic difficulty adjustments and recommendation systems that suggest games based on player preferences.

In the realm of tabletop gaming, particularly in RPGs AI's role is more nuanced and is just beginning to be fully explored. Here, AI serves as a creative partner for the game master, helping to flesh out intricate worlds and complex characters. It can generate content ranging from detailed descriptions of environments to entire questlines, complete with plots, NPCs, and dialogue options. AI tools can assist with rules management, quickly calculate outcomes, and provide suggestions for encounter balancing, leaving GMs free to focus on the narrative and player engagement.

The overarching promise of AI in gaming, and particularly for tabletop RPGs, is to act as a force multiplier for human creativity, enabling more immersive, expansive, and personalized gaming experiences. As technology continues to advance, the role of AI in gaming is set to become more innovative, providing tools that could redefine the boundaries of interactive storytelling.

As I delve deeper into the craft of game mastery, I've begun experimenting with a new tool that feels as though it is straight out of a wizard's tome: ChatGPT. I approach it with the curiosity of a mage exploring a newly discovered spell, cautious yet eager to see what creative alchemy we can conjure together.

My first foray into this partnership was with character dialogue. I'd type out the skeleton of a conversation, and ChatGPT would breathe life into it, clothing the bare bones in flesh and personality. I marveled as the voices of my characters gained texture and depth, their words flowing with an authenticity that sometimes even I hadn't anticipated. It was like having a troupe of actors at my fingertips, each ready to recite lines in perfect cadence with their roles.

Next, I tasked ChatGPT with scene descriptions. I would provide a framework: a misty forest at dawn, the cacophony of a bustling marketplace, or the oppressive silence of an ancient tomb.

ChatGPT would then fill in the sensory details, painting with words so vivid that I could almost hear the leaves rustling and feel the eerie chill of the crypt. It was a revelation to watch my worlds grow richer and more immersive, simply through the power of well-chosen words.

Perhaps most intriguing has been using ChatGPT to flesh out the features of fantasy races. I would supply the seed of an idea—a race of subterranean creatures sensitive to light, or aerial beings dwelling in the highest mountain peaks. ChatGPT would then help me expand these concepts, suggesting physiological traits, cultural quirks, and historical backgrounds. It was like having an oracle to consult, one that could see the potential in every seed I planted and help it grow into a fully-formed idea.

Through all this, I've come to see ChatGPT not just as a tool, but as a collaborator in the creative process. It's a source of inspiration that's endlessly patient, ready to assist me in bringing the worlds in my mind into the shared reality of the game table. With each session, I learn more about its capabilities and limitations, and with each discovery, I find myself more excited about the future of AI in tabletop gaming. It's a journey of constant learning, but one that's deeply rewarding, as I watch my games come alive in ways I never thought possible.

I recently had an idea for a possum folk ancestry. I decided that they should have a feature similar but contrasting with the Orc's Relentless Endurance. Instead of triggering at zero HP, it would fake death at 1 HP. So, I put this prompt in ChatGPT 4.0:

"Create a racial feature for a possum folk race, in which the possum goes unconscious at 1 HP for self-preservation. Give it a cool name, preferably a pun."

Here is the first Possum Folk ability:

Ability: Prehensile Pretense

Feature Description: Among the possum folk, there is an ancient and instinctive trait that's been honed for self-preservation, known as "Prehensile Pretense." When a possum folk's vitality is hanging by a thread, teetering at the brink of unconsciousness, they can invoke this racial feature. If a possum folk is reduced to 1 hit point, they automatically tap into their ancestral survival tactics, playing dead with such convincing flair that even the most discerning predator would be duped.

Upon activation of Prehensile Pretense, the possum folk's body goes limp, their breathing becomes shallow, and they exude a scent that mimics the olfactory signature of a deceased creature. To any onlooker, the possum folk appears utterly lifeless. During this feigned death, they are incapacitated and can observe their surroundings without moving or making a sound. This state lasts until they choose to end it (as a minor action on their turn), until they are healed or harmed, or until a minute has passed.

The Prehensile Pretense can only be used once, recharging after the possum folk has finished a long rest. This feature not only provides a crucial moment of reprieve in the heat of battle but can also turn the tide, allowing the possum folk and their allies to mount a counterattack or make a strategic retreat.

Then I figured my Possum Folk could use that prehensile tail for something, maybe just an extra interaction per turn. So I put this to ChatGPT 4.0:

"Now create another racial trait in which the Possum folk can use their prehensile tail for an extra interact."

Ability: Tail Of Utility

Feature Description: The possum folk are renowned for their

dexterity and adaptability, traits epitomized by their racial ability known as "Tail of Utility." Their prehensile tail functions as a versatile appendage capable of gripping, holding, and manipulating objects with a surprising degree of precision.

As part of this racial trait, a possum folk can use their tail to perform tasks that would normally require a free hand. This includes, but is not limited to, holding a light item, opening an unlocked door, retrieving a small object from an open pack, or even pouring the contents from a vial.

Once per turn, a possum folk can perform an additional "interact with an object" action without using their hands, thanks to their adept tail. This does not count against the usual number of interactions a creature can perform on their turn, effectively giving the possum folk an extra layer of utility in various scenarios.

The Tail of Utility is a testament to the possum folk's evolutionary ingenuity, allowing them to engage with their environment in unique ways that can provide creative solutions to challenges and add an unexpected edge in and out of combat.

As you can see, the AI quickly completed the task of describing the Possum Folk's unique abilities just as I had envisioned, but much faster than I would have. In fact, I am sure I would have fiddled for hours over those two bits of texts. Using ChatGPT freed me from the strain of writing and thrust me into full on creativity.

I hesitate to touch on other uses of AI, as I feel there is still much to be learned and ethics to be considered. Using AI to generate visual art, for instance like the cover of this first edition, does trouble me. In fact, I will be commissioning a human artist for the cover of the next edition due to my beliefs that artists deserve to be paid.

CHAPTER 24:
CURTAINS!

As we draw the final curtain on this comprehensive journey through the art and science of being a professional game master, it's essential to recognize that the end of this book is merely the beginning of your adventure. The landscapes you will craft, the stories you will weave, and the experiences you will facilitate are bound only by the limits of your imagination and the breadth of your dedication.

In this tome, we've traversed the foundational stones of game mastering—from crafting compelling narratives and managing dynamic group dynamics to mastering the mechanics of gameplay and creating immersive experiences. Each chapter has been a step towards honing your skills, refining your craft, and understanding the profound responsibility that comes with guiding players through the realms of fantasy and beyond.

Remember, the path of a professional game master is one of continuous learning and adaptation. The strategies and techniques discussed here are your starting gear, but the quests for knowledge and improvement never truly end. Embrace each gaming session as an opportunity to experiment, learn, and

HOW TO BE A PROFESSIONAL GAME MASTER

evolve. Reflect on what worked and what did not—every table is unique, and every experience is a treasure trove of insights.

For those who thirst for deeper wells of knowledge, the appendix of this book holds a trove of further resources. There, you will find a curated list of books, online communities, tools, and references that will serve as your companions and guides as you delve deeper into the caverns of game mastery. Engage with these resources, connect with fellow game masters, and partake in the collective wisdom of a community that thrives on shared stories and experiences.

As your journey continues, keep the core tenets close to your heart—fairness, creativity, adaptability, and respect for your players. Remember that being a professional game master is not just about leading a game, but also about uplifting and inspiring your players, crafting memories that resonate beyond the table, and creating worlds that linger in the imagination long after the dice have settled.

Now, turn the page, set the scene, and let the dice fall where they may. Your story is just beginning.

Until our paths cross again at the table, may your narratives be rich and your adventures legendary.

RESOURCES

Here is a brief but very important list of resources for every professional game master. There are countless more resources to discover, but these are my essentials.

GAME MASTER RESOURCES

The Lazy Dm

https://slyflourish.com/lazydm/

Donjon Rpg Tools

https://donjon.bin.sh/

Matthew Colville's Excellent Youtube Series, Running The Game

https://www.youtube.com/@mcolville

My Favorite Episode "Problem Players":

https://www.youtube.com/watch?v=-lEi9DAn9rE

CHARACTER CREATION

Sly Flourish's Fiasco Style Bonds:

https://slyflourish.com/fiasco_relationships.html

D&D Bonds By Skullsplitter Dice

https://www.skullsplitterdice.com/blogs/dnd/5e-bonds

SAFETY TOOLS

Ttrpg Safety Toolkit

http://bit.ly/ttrpgsafetytoolkit

The X Card By John Stavropoulus

http://tinyurl.com/x-card-rpg

Monte Cook's Consent In Gaming Includes A Checklist That You Can Use In Your Session Zero:

https://www.montecookgames.com/consent-in-gaming/

The Value Of Line And Veils

https://adventurerules.blog/2018/01/15/the-value-of-lines-and-veils/

Script Change Rpg Toolbox

https://thoughty.itch.io/script-change

Accessibility In Gaming By Jennifer Kretchmer

https://docs.google.com/document/d/1ZFSXz-Yva1KZAsP7NblCdkoiQ6RcjxSV2gj98eXusJs/edit

AUTHOR'S BIOGRAPHY

David Cusack is a seasoned grognard with more than four decades of experience in the realm of tabletop role-playing games. He caught the D&D bug early when he stumbled upon the Greyhawk supplement in a strange corner of the local hobby shop. From 1978 to 1981, he delved into dungeons and slayed monsters sitting at a ping-pong table become battlefield, in a basement with musty shag carpeting, much like those kids in the beloved series "Stranger Things."

After a time, David explored the world of 2nd edition Advanced Dungeons & Dragons, then moved to Traveller, GURPS, and a plethora of other tabletop RPGs, finding his way back home to D&D with the advent of its 5th Edition. A tech-savvy enthusiast, he's particularly passionate about the opportunities that virtual tabletops like Roll20 offer. David blends his old-school Dungeon Master style with modern technology.

His fervor for teaching shines through in his sessions. He aims to provide a thrilling in-game experience and takes immense pleasure in introducing newbies to the 5th Edition of D&D and the nuances of playing on virtual platforms like Roll20.

As a professional Dungeon Master, David has run over 600 sessions, helmed ten long-term campaigns that reached the zenith of level 20, and guided over 250 players through their own epic tales. With this book, he distills his extensive experience into invaluable insights and best practices, aiming to elevate the craft of Game Mastering to new heights. Whether you're a seasoned GM looking to go pro or a newbie aspiring to wield the DM's screen, David's expertise offers something for everyone.

www.ingramcontent.com/pod-product-compliance
Lightning Source LLC
Chambersburg PA
CBHW072204290526
45794CB00004B/1639

*9 7 9 8 8 6 6 4 4 1 8 6 0 *